instant
SPANISH

Elisabeth Smith

D0721024

TEACH YOURSELF BOOKS

There is a cassette (ISBN: 0 340 70505 1) available to accompany this book. If you experience problems obtaining it from your bookseller please contact Bookpoint Ltd, 130 Milton Park, Abingdon, Oxon OX14 4SB. Telephone: (44) 01235 400414, Fax: (44) 01235 400454. Lines are open from 9.00–6.00, Monday to Saturday, with a 24 hour message answering service. E-mail address: orders@bookpoint.co.uk

For U.S.A. order enquiries: please contact McGraw-Hill Customer Services, P.O Box 545, Blacklick, OH 43004-0545, U.S.A. Telephone: 1-800-722-4726. Fax: 1-614-755-5645.

For Canada order enquiries: please contact McGraw-Hill Ryerson Ltd., 300 Water St, Whitby, Ontario L1N 9B6, Canada. Telephone: 905 430 5000. Fax: 905 430 5020.

Long renowned as the authoritative source for self-guided learning – with more than 30 million copies sold worldwide – the *Teach Yourself* series includes over 300 titles in the fields of languages, crafts, hobbies, business and education.

British Library Cataloguing in Publication Data
A catalogue entry for this title is available from The British Library.

Library of Congress Catalog Card Number: On file

First published in UK 1998 by Hodder Headline Plc, 338 Euston Road, London, NW1 3BH.

First published in US 1998 by Contemporary Books, A Division of The McGraw-Hill Companies, 4255 West Touhy Avenue, Lincolnwood (Chicago), Illinois 60712-1975 U.S.A.

The 'Teach Yourself' name and logo are registered trade marks of Hodder & Stoughton Ltd.

Typeset by Transet Limited, Coventry, England.
Printed in Great Britain for Hodder & Stoughton Educational, a division of Hodder Headline Plc, 338 Euston Road, London NW1 3BH by Cox & Wyman Ltd, Reading, Berkshire.

Impression number   14
Year   2002, 2001

CONTENTS

HOW THIS
BOOK WORKS

INSTANT **Spanish** has been structured for your rapid success.
This is how it works:

DAY-BY-DAY GUIDE Stick to it. If you miss a day, add one.

DIALOGUES Follow Tom and Kate through Spain. The English of Weeks 1–3 is in 'Spanish-speak' to get you tuned in.

NEW WORDS Don't fight them, don't skip them – learn them! The Flash cards will help you.

GOOD NEWS GRAMMAR After you read it you can forget half and still succeed! That's why it's Good News.

FLASH WORDS AND FLASH SENTENCES Read about these building blocks in the Flash card section on page 64. Then use them!

LEARN BY HEART Obligatory! Memorizing puts you on the fast track to speaking in full sentences.

LET'S SPEAK SPANISH *You* will be doing the talking – in Spanish.

SPOT THE KEYS Listen to rapid Spanish and make sense of it.

SAY IT SIMPLY Learn how to use plain, *INSTANT* **Spanish** to say what you want to say. Don't be shy!

TEST YOUR PROGRESS Mark your own test and be amazed by the result.

This is where you find the answers to the exercises.

This icon asks you to switch on the tape.

PRONUNCIATION If you don't know it and don't have the tape go straight to page 11. You need to know the pronunciation before you can start Week 1.

Progress Chart Enter your score each week and monitor your progress. Are you going for *very good* or *outstanding*?

Certificate It's on the last page. In six weeks it will have your name on it!

READD THIS FIRST

If, like me, you usually skip introductions – don't turn the page. Read on! You need to know how *INSTANT* **Spanish** works and why.

When I decided to write the *INSTANT* series I first called it *Barebones*, because that's what you want: *no frills, no fuss, just the bare bones and go!* So in *INSTANT* **Spanish** you'll find:

- Only 390 words to say all, well ... nearly all.
- No ghastly grammar – just a few useful tips.
- No time wasters such as 'the pen of my aunt...'.
- No phrase book phrases for when you take Flamenco lessons in Bilbao.
- No need to be perfect. Mistakes won't spoil your success.

I put some 30 years of teaching experience into this course. I know how people learn. I also know for how long they are motivated by a new project (a few weeks) and how little time they can spare to study each day (½ hour). That's why you'll complete *INSTANT* **Spanish** in six weeks and get away with 35 minutes a day.

Of course there is some learning to do, but I have tried to make it as much fun as possible, even when it is boring. You'll meet Tom and Kate Walker on holiday in Spain. They do the kind of things you need to know about: shopping, eating out and getting about. As you will note Tom and Kate speak *INSTANT* **Spanish** all the time, even to each other. What paragons of virtue!

There are only two things you must do:
- Follow the Day-by-Day Guide as suggested. Please don't skip bits and short-change your success. Everything is there for a reason.
- Please buy the cassette that accompanies this book. It will also get you to speak faster and with confidence.

When you have filled in your Certificate at the end of the book and can speak *INSTANT* **Spanish**, I would like to hear from you. You can write to me care of Hodder & Stoughton Educational.

Elizabeth Smith

PROGRESS CHART

At the end of each week record your test score on the Progress Chart below.

At the end of the course throw out your worst result – everybody can have a bad week – and add up your *five* best weekly scores. Divide the total by five to get your average score and overall course result. Write your result – *outstanding*, *excellent*, *very good* or *good* – on your Certificate.

If you scored more than 80% enlarge it and frame it!

PROGRESS CHART

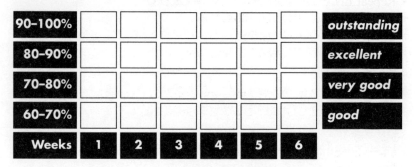

90–100%							*outstanding*
80–90%							*excellent*
70–80%							*very good*
60–70%							*good*
Weeks	1	2	3	4	5	6	

TOTAL OF FIVE BEST WEEKS _____

DIVIDED BY FIVE =

YOUR FINAL RESULT _____%

1 | WEEK ONE DAY-BY-DAY GUIDE

Study for 35 minutes – or a little longer if you can!

Day Zero
• Start with READ THIS FIRST!
• Read HOW THIS BOOK WORKS.

Day One
• Read IN THE AEROPLANE.
• Listen to/Read EN EL AVIÓN.
• Listen to/Read the NEW WORDS, then learn some of them.

Day Two
• Repeat EN EL AVIÓN and NEW WORDS.
• Listen to/Read PRONUNCIATION.
• Learn more NEW WORDS.
• Use the FLASH WORDS to help you.

Day Three
• Learn all NEW WORDS until you know them well.
• Read and learn GOOD NEWS GRAMMAR.

Day Four
• Cut out and learn the 10 FLASH SENTENCES.
• Listen to/Read LEARN BY HEART.

Day Five
• Listen to/Read LET'S SPEAK SPANISH.
• Revise! Tomorrow you'll be testing your progress.

Day Six
• Translate TEST YOUR PROGRESS.

Day Seven This is your day off!

∞ IN THE AEROPLANE

Tom and Kate Walker are on their way to Spain. They are boarding flight QS 915 to Malaga via Barcelona and squeeze past Pedro Iglesias.

Tom   Excuse me, we have the seats four a and four b.

Pedro   Ah, yes, a moment please.

Tom   Hello, how are you? We are Tom and Kate Walker.

Pedro   Good morning, I call myself (My name is) Iglesias.

Tom   Julio Iglesias?

Pedro   No, come off it! My name is Pedro Iglesias.

Tom   We are going to Malaga. And you?

Pedro   No, I am going to Barcelona but I am from Seville.

Tom   Seville? I was in Seville in May – for my company.

Pedro   In what do you work?

Tom   I work with computers.

Pedro   And you, Mrs Walker?

Kate   Well... I have worked in Mobil three years. Now I work in Rover.

Pedro   Are you from London?

Kate   No, we are from Manchester. We have been one year in New York and two years in London. Now we work in Birmingham.

Pedro   I have worked four years in Seat but now I work in the Bank of Spain.

Tom   And how is the work in the bank? Is it good?

Pedro   The work is boring but the pay is better. I have a house big, a Mercedes and four children. My wife is American from Los Angeles and she has a girlfriend in Dallas. She talks always with her on the telephone and goes always to Los Angeles. It costs a lot of money.

Kate   And are you now also on holiday?

Pedro   No, unfortunately not. We have always the holidays in September. We are going to Mallorca but without the children. We have a house in Palma and – without telephone!

🔊 📼 EN EL AVIÓN

Tom and Kate Walker are on their way to Spain. They are boarding flight QS 915 to Malaga via Barcelona and squeeze past Pedro Iglesias.

Tom   Perdone, tenemos los asientos cuatro a y cuatro b.

Pedro   ¡Ah! sí, un momento por favor.

Tom   Hola, ¿Qué tal? Somos Tom y Kate Walker.

Pedro   Buenos días. Me llamo Iglesias.

Tom   ¿Julio Iglesias?

Pedro   No, ¡qué va! Me llamo Pedro Iglesias.

Tom   Nosotros vamos a Málaga. ¿Y usted?

Pedro   No, yo voy a Barcelona pero soy de Sevilla.

Tom   ¿Sevilla? He estado en Sevilla en mayo – para mi empresa.

Pedro   ¿En qué trabaja?

Tom   Trabajo con ordenadores.

Pedro   ¿Y usted, señora Walker?

Kate   Pues... yo he trabajado en Mobil tres años. Ahora trabajo en Rover.

Pedro   ¿Es de Londres?

Kate   No, somos de Manchester. Hemos estado un año en Nueva York y dos años en Londres. Ahora trabajamos en Birmingham.

Pedro   Yo he trabajado cuatro años en Seat pero ahora trabajo en el Banco de España.

Tom   ¿Y qué tal el trabajo en el banco? ¿Es bueno?

Pedro   El trabajo es aburrido pero el sueldo es mejor. Tengo una casa grande, un Mercedes y cuatro niños. Mi mujer es americana, de Los Angeles, y tiene una amiga en Dallas. Habla siempre con ella por teléfono y va siempre a Los Angeles. Cuesta mucho dinero.

Kate   ¿Y está ahora también de vacaciones?

Pedro   No, desgraciadamente no. Tenemos siempre las vacaciones en septiembre. Vamos a Mallorca, pero sin los niños. Tenemos una casa en Palma y – ¡sin teléfono!

abcd... 📼 NEW WORDS

Learning words the traditional way can be boring. If you enjoy the FLASH CARDS why not make your own for the rest of the words. Always say the words ALOUD. It's the fast track to speaking!

en *in / on*
el, la, los, las *the*
el avión *the aeroplane*
perdone, perdón *excuse me*
tenemos *we have*
los asientos *the seats*
cuatro *four*
a, b pronounced **'uh', 'bay'**
y *and*
sí *yes*
un momento *a moment*
por favor *please*
hola *hello*
¿qué tal? *how are you, how is…?*
somos *we are*
buenos días *good day, good morning*
me llamo *my name is…*
no *no, not*
¡qué va! *come on!* (expression)
nosotros *we*
vamos *we go, we are going, let's go!*
a/al *to, to the*
usted/ustedes *you* (one person) */ you* (more than one person)
yo *I*
voy *I go, I am going*
pero *but*
soy *I am*
de/del *from, of / from, of the*
he estado *I have been, I was*
mayo *May*
para *for*

mi *my*
la empresa *the company*
qué *what*
trabaja *he/she/it works, you work*
trabajo *I work,* also: *(the) work*
con *with*
ordenador/es *computer/s*
señora *Mrs, woman*
pues… *well…, well then*
he trabajado *I have worked*
tres *three*
el año, los años *the year, the years*
ahora *now*
es *you are, he/she / it is*
hemos estado *we have been, we were*
un, una *a, one*
dos *two*
trabajamos *we work*
el Banco de España *the Bank of Spain*
bueno/a *good*
aburrido/a *boring*
el sueldo *the pay, salary*
mejor *better*
tengo *I have*
una casa / en casa *a house / at home*
grande *big*
los niños *the children*
la mujer *the woman, wife*
americana *American*
tiene *he/she/it has, you have*

una amiga *a girlfriend*	**mucho/a** *much, a lot*
habla *he/she/it speaks, you speak*	**el dinero** *the money*
siempre *always*	**está** *he/she/it is, you are*
ella *she, her*	**también** *also*
por teléfono *on the telephone*	**de vacaciones** *on holiday(s)*
va *he/she/it goes, you go*	**desgraciadamente** *unfortunately*
cuesta/cuestan *it costs /*	**septiembre** *September*
they cost	**sin** *without*

TOTAL NEW WORDS: 75
...only 315 words to go!

Some easy extras

los meses (the months)

enero, febrero, marzo, abril, mayo, junio, julio, agosto, septiembre, octubre, noviembre, diciembre

Numeros (numbers)

cero,	uno,	dos,	tres,	cuatro,	cinco,	seis,	siete,	ocho,	nueve,	diez
0	1	2	3	4	5	6	7	8	9	10

More greetings

buenas tardes (*good afternoon*), **buenas noches** (*good night*), **hasta luego** (*bye, until later*) **adiós** (*good bye, for longer absence*).

⬛ PRONUNCIATION

The Spanish language is beautiful, so drop all inhibitions and try to speak **Spanish** – not English with the words changed…!

If the Spanish pronunciation is new to you please buy the cassette. But if you are good at languages, or would like a refresher, here are the rules:

First the vowels

The word in brackets gives you an example of the sound. Say the sound ALOUD and then the Spanish examples ALOUD.

a	(*star*)	c**a**sa, M**á**laga, d**í**as, **v**amos
e	(*yes*)	**e**s, p**e**ro, bu**e**no, tel**é**fono
i	(*field*)	s**í**, s**i**n, m**i**, d**í**as, as**i**entos
o	(*no*)	n**o**, c**o**n, s**o**m**o**s, m**o**ment**o**
u	(*June*)	**u**n, **u**sted, c**u**esta, m**u**cho

All vowels are pronounced separately: b**u**–**e**–no, as**i**–**en**–tos

Consonants

h (-)		This is not pronounced at all.
		hola, **h**e, **h**emos, **h**abla, a**h**ora
j (*loch*)		Like the guttural sound in the Scottish word lo**ch**.
		Julio, traba**j**o, mu**j**er
ll (*yes/million*)		It is a bit of each.
		When you say me **ll**amo the **ll** sounds like a **y**, but when you say ca**ll**e it's more like the **ll** in mi**ll**ion. If your tongue gives up, stay with the **y**. Say: a**ll**í, Sevi**ll**a
ñ (*canyon*)		Watch out when you see the little wriggle on the top of the **n**. A**ñ**o, ni**ñ**o, (say a**ny**o, ni**ny**o) Espa**ñ**a
qu (*kettle*)		**qu**é, **qu**ince (15), **qu**inientos (500)
r		Give this a vigorous, throaty roll abu**rrr**ido…
z (*this*)		The moment you spot a **z**, it's a lisp.
		cerve**z**a (beer), i**z**quierda (left), tro**z**o (piece)

c This comes in two guises

ca	(*cat*)	
co	(*cot*)	This part is easy, and is just like the English!
cu	(*cut*)	**c**asa, **c**on, **c**uatro, **c**laro (clear)
c + consonant	(*clear*)	
ce	(*theft*)	A **c** before an **e** or an **i**, it's a sharp lisp!
ci	(*thick*)	Bar**c**elona, **c**inco, desgra**c**iadamente

The **g** is equally fanciful. It comes in four varieties!

ga	(*gag*)	
go	(*go*)	Easy! Just like the English!
gu	(*gust*)	**g**rande, **g**olf, **g**uapo
g + consonant	(*grand*)	
ge, gi	(lo**ch**)	It's back to the throaty **ch** of lo**ch**!
		Luckily, there are only two *INSTANT* words with **ge** or **gi**, **g**ente and cole**g**io.

The accent – always stress the second syllable from the end: mo-**men**-to, tra-**ba**-jo, te-**ne**-mos, or-de-na-**do**-res. When there's an accent stress that part: **te-lé**-fo-no.

Congratulations for having worked through the rules of pronunciation!

◉ GOOD NEWS GRAMMAR

This is the GOOD NEWS part of each lesson. Remember, I promised: *no ghastly grammar!* Every week I explain just a few things and talk you through the differences between English and Spanish. This will help you to speak Spanish *INSTANTly*.

1 - Names of things – nouns

There are two kinds of nouns in Spanish: masculine and feminine. You can tell which is which by the word **el** or **la**, or **un** or **una** in front of the word. You can also tell by the ending of the noun.

Words ending in **-o** are masculine: **El** diner**o** or **un** banc**o**,
Words ending in **-a** are feminine: **La** cas**a** or **una** amig**a**

The adjective describing a noun also ends in **-o** or **-a**. So the *good* bank or house becomes: **la casa buena** or **un banco bueno**.

Unfortunately, not all nouns and adjectives behave so obediently. Some nouns end in any old letter: la muje**r** or la televisió**n** (the TV), and some adjectives, like **grande**, do not change. And then there is **el** día, just to confuse you!

But these non-conformists are in the minority, so most of the time you can get it right … el dinero bueno … una amiga buena.

When there is more than one thing (plural) **el** becomes **los**. All the rest just add an **s**. Los banc**os** buen**os**, las amig**as** buen**as**.

Good news: If you get muddled and say **los** cas**as** buen**os** nobody is going to throw a fit. Everyone will understand you perfectly!

2 - Doing things – verbs

This is a bit of bad news in Spanish, so brace yourself!
Unlike the English, the Spanish do not use **I, you, he, she, it, we,** or **they** to identify **who** is doing something unless they wish to clarify or stress it. So most of the time the only way you can tell **who is doing something** is by the **verb itself**.

Each person has his/her own form of verb ending, but sometimes an ending is shared. This could lead to some confusion, but amazingly it usually works out all right.

There are a handful of verbs which you'll need every day. Spend 10 minutes on each. **Trabajar** belongs to the good verbs team. Team members have the same endings. Know one – know all!

	trabajar: *(to) work*		**tener:** *(to) have*	
(yo)	**trabajo**	I work	**tengo**	I have
(usted)	**trabaja**	you work	**tiene**	you have
(él)	**trabaja**	he, it works	**tiene**	he, it has
(ella)	**trabaja**	she, it works	**tiene**	she, it has
(nosotros)	**trabajamos**	we work	**tenemos**	we have
(ellos, ellas)	**trabajan**	they work	**tienen**	they have
(ustedes)	**trabajan**	you work	**tienen**	you have

(usted) **trabaja** – (ustedes) **trabajan**: **trabaja** is used when talking to one person, **trabajan**, when talking to more than one. **¿Trabaja, Kate? ¿Trabajan, Tom y Kate?** Are you shell-shocked? Will you remember all these endings? Don't worry! By Week 3 it will be a piece of cake!

3 - Asking questions

Es bueno. It is good. ¿Es bueno? Is it good? You simply use your voice to turn a statement into a question.

♥ 📼 LEARN BY HEART

Don't be tempted to skip this exercise because it reminds you of school... If you want to SPEAK, not stumble, saying a few lines by HEART does the trick! Learn ME LLAMO by heart after you have filled in the gaps with your personal, or any, information.

Example Me llamo Sarah Lawson. Soy de Newcastle.

When you know the lines by heart, go over them again until you can say them aloud fluently and fairly fast. Can you beat 40 seconds? Excellent! Give **Me llamo** a bit of life. You'll remember it better that way.

ME LLAMO...
Me llamo ....(name).
Soy de..(place).
He estado en ....(place) en.................... (month).
He trabajado en ....(name of firm) tres años.
Ahora trabajo en..(name of firm).
Tengo una casa en ....(place) y cuesta mucho.
En agosto vamos a...(place).
¿Qué tal Marbella en enero, bueno o aburrido?

◯ ⬚ *LET'S SPEAK SPANISH!*

If you have the cassette, close the book and listen to LET'S SPEAK SPANISH. If you do not have the cassette, read on.

I shall give you ten English sentences and you'll put them into Spanish. Always speak ALOUD. After each one check the answer at the bottom of this page. Tick it if you got it right.

1	Hello, my name is Walker.	6	Do you have a Mercedes?
2	Are you from London?	7	No, unfortunately not.
3	Yes, I am from London.	8	We have a house in Marbella.
4	We are going home. Bye!	9	How is the work, good?
5	I work with Pedro in Palma.	10	Boring, but the pay is good.

Well, how many did you get right? If you are not happy do it again?

*Here are some questions in Spanish and you are going to answer in Spanish. Answer the first five with **sí**, and talk about yourself. In questions 16–20 I am talking to you and your friend. Say **sí** and we.*

11 ¿Es de Bristol?
12 ¿Tiene una casa en Londres?
13 Pepe va a Granada. ¿Y usted?
14 ¿Tiene un teléfono?
15 ¿Trabaja con ordenadores?
16 Vamos a casa. ¿Y ustedes?
17 Trabajamos en Los Angeles. ¿Y ustedes?
18 Tenemos amigos en Málaga. ¿Y ustedes?
19 Vamos a Sevilla. ¿Y ustedes?
20 Tenemos un trabajo aburrido. ¿Y ustedes?

Answers to LET'S SPEAK SPANISH

1	Hola, me llamo Walker.	11	Sí, soy de Bristol.
2	Es de Londres?	12	Sí, tengo una casa en Londres.
3	Sí, soy de Londres.	13	Sí, voy a Granada.
4	Vamos a casa. ¡Hasta luego!	14	Sí, tengo un teléfono.
5	Trabajo con Pedro en Palma.	15	Sí, trabajo con ordenadores.
6	¿Tiene un Mercedes?	16	Sí, vamos a casa.
7	No, desgraciadamente, no.	17	Sí, trabajamos en Los Angeles.
8	Tenemos una casa en Marbella.	18	Sí, tenemos amigos en Málaga.
9	¿Qué tal el trabajo, bueno?	19	Sí, vamos a Sevilla.
10	Aburrido, pero el sueldo es bueno.	20	Sí, tenemos un trabajo aburrido.

Well, what was your score? If you ticked all of them, give yourself ★ ★ ★!

☑☒ TEST YOUR PROGRESS

This is your only **written** exercise. You'll be amazed at how easy it is! Translate the 20 sentences without looking at the previous pages. The bits in brackets tell you how it is said in Spanish.

1 My name is Peter Smith.
2 Hello, we are Helen and Pepe.
3 I am from Toledo. And you?
4 Maria is a good friend.
5 I always go home in June.
6 We work in Alicante in August.
7 Do you always go to New York in March?
8 What work do you do? (In what do you work?) Do you work with computers?
9 She is in London with the children.
10 One moment, please. What is it? Does it cost a lot?
11 Does the house have a telephone? No, unfortuantely not.
12 Good day, are you (the) Mrs Lopez from Madrid?
13 I work without pay at an American company.
14 Now I have a better job. I work for three big banks.
15 Paco! How are you? Are we going to Seville?
16 My wife is also American. She is from Boston.
17 We have good seats in the aeroplane.
18 Do I have a Mercedes? Come off it!
19 My girlfriend speaks Spanish (español), but not a lot.
20 I am going on holiday with Carmen. Unfortunately she is boring.

When you have finished look up the answers on page 60, and mark your work. Then enter your result on the Progress Chart on page 6. If your score is higher than 80% you'll have done very well indeed!

2 WEEK TWO DAY-BY-DAY GUIDE

35 minutes a day – but a little extra will step up your progress!

Day One
- Read IN THE SIERRA NEVADA.
- Listen to/Read EN SIERRA NEVADA.
- Listen to/Read NEW WORDS. Learn 20 easy ones.

Day Two
- Repeat EN SIERRA NEVADA and NEW WORDS.
- Go over PRONUNCIATION.
- Learn the harder NEW WORDS.
- Use the FLASH WORDS to help you.

Day Three
- Learn all NEW WORDS until you know them well.
- Read and learn GOOD NEWS GRAMMAR.

Day Four
- Cut out and learn the FLASH SENTENCES.
- Listen to/Read LEARN BY HEART.

Day Five
- Listen to/Read LET'S SPEAK SPANISH.
- Go over NO TENGO MUCHO DINERO, PERO…

Day Six
- Translate TEST YOUR PROGRESS.

Day Seven
This is a study-free day!

⊂⊃ IN SIERRA NEVADA

In Malaga Tom and Kate hire a car and drive to the Sierra Nevada. They speak to Rita López of "Casa Margarita", and later to Paco, the waiter.

Kate Good afternoon. Have you a room double for one night and not very expensive, please?

Rita Yes, I have a room small with bathroom. But the shower is broken. My husband it can repair tomorrow.

Tom Right, where is the room?

Rita Here on the left. Not it is very big.

Kate The room is a little small but nice. How much does it cost?

Rita Only 6,000 pesetas but we do not take credit cards. There is a big breakfast from eight to ten and half.

Kate All right, we take the room. But can we take the breakfast at eight less quarter? We would like to go to Marbella tomorrow at eight and quarter.

Rita Agreed.

Kate Can I ask you where we can we take coffee? Is there near here a cafeteria.....or a bar? Where are they?

Rita It is very easy. There is a cafeteria at five minutes from here, at some 30 metres on the right and then straight ahead.

(In the cafeteria)

Paco What would you like to take, please?

Kate We would like a coffee with milk and a tea, please.

Paco And something to eat? We have snacks, omelette, toast....

Tom Right,...two toasts, please

Tom The table is not clean.

Kate Yes, but the cafeteria is not bad.

Tom My tea is cold.

Kate Yes, but the toilets are great.

Tom The toast is bad.

Kate Yes, but the waiter is very handsome.

Tom The bill, please.

Paco 850 pesetas, please.

🔊 📼 EN SIERRA NEVADA

In Malaga Tom and Kate hire a car and drive to the Sierra Nevada. They speak to Rita López of "Casa Margarita", and later to Paco, the waiter.

Kate Buenas tardes, ¿tiene usted una habitación doble para una noche y no muy cara, por favor?

Rita Sí, tengo una habitación pequeña con cuarto de baño. Pero la ducha está rota. Mi marido la puede reparar mañana.

Tom Bueno, ¿dónde está la habitación?

Rita Aquí, a la izquierda. No es muy grande.

Kate La habitación es un poco pequeña pero bonita. ¿Cuánto cuesta?

Rita Sólo seis mil pesetas, pero no tomamos tarjetas de crédito. Hay un gran desayuno de ocho a diez y media.

Kate Vale, tomamos la habitación. Pero, ¿podemos tomar el desayuno a las ocho menos cuarto? Quisiéramos ir a Marbella mañana a las ocho y cuarto.

Rita De acuerdo.

Kate ¿Puedo preguntarle dónde podemos tomar café? ¿Hay aquí cerca una cafetería ...o un bar? ¿Dónde están?

Rita Es muy fácil. Hay una cafetería a cinco minutos de aquí, a unos treinta metros a la derecha y luego todo recto.

(En la cafetería)

Paco ¿Qué desean tomar, por favor?

Kate Quisiéramos un café con leche y un té, por favor.

Paco Y ¿algo para comer? Tenemos tapas, tortilla, tostadas....

Tom Bueno, ...dos tostadas por favor.

Tom La mesa no está limpia.

Kate Sí, pero la cafetería no es mala.

Tom Mi té está frío.

Kate Sí, pero los servicios son estupendos.

Tom La tostada está mala.

Kate Sí, pero el camarero es muy guapo.

Tom La cuenta, por favor.

Paco Ochocientas cincuenta pesetas, por favor.

abcd... 📼 NEW WORDS

una habitación doble *a double room*	**puedo** *I can*
una noche *a night*	**preguntar** *to ask*
muy *very*	**¿puedo preguntarle?** *Can I ask you?*
caro/a *expensive*	**café** *coffee*
pequeño/a *small*	**cerca** *near*
el cuarto de baño *the bathroom*	**una cafetería** *a café*
la ducha *the shower*	**o** *or*
roto/a *broken*	**están** *they are, you are* (plural)
el marido *the husband*	**fácil** *easy*
lo, la (by itself) *it*	**minutos** *minutes*
puede *he, she can, you can*	**unos, unas** *some*
reparar *(to) repair*	**treinta metros** *thirty metres*
mañana *tomorrow*	**a la derecha** *on the right*
bueno/a (by itself) *all right, right*	**luego** *then, later*
dónde *where*	**todo recto** *straight ahead*
aquí *here*	**¿qué desean?** *what do you wish?*
a la izquierda *on the left*	**la leche** *the milk*
un poco *a little*	**un té** *a tea*
bonito/a *pretty, lovely*	**algo** *something*
cuánto *how much…?*	**comer** *(to) eat*
sólo *only*	**¿qué tienen ustedes?** *What do you have?*
mil *thousand*	**tapas** *Spanish snacks*
pesetas *Spanish currency*	**una tortilla** *a Spanish omelette*
las tarjetas de crédito *the credit cards*	**tostadas** *toast*
el desayuno *the breakfast*	**la mesa** *the table*
hay *there is*	**limpio/a** *clean*
medio *half*	**frío/a** *cold*
vale *all right, OK*	**malo/a** *bad*
tomamos *we'll take*	**los servicios** *the toilets*
tomar *to take*	**son** *are, they are*
podemos *we can*	**estupendo/a** *marvellous, great*
menos *less*	**el camarero** *the waiter*
cuarto *quarter*	**guapo/a** *good-looking*
quisiéramos *we would like (to)*	**la cuenta** *the bill*
ir *(to) go*	**ochocientas cincuenta** *850*
de acuerdo *agreed, OK*	

TOTAL NEW WORDS: 73
...only 242 words to go!

⊙ *GOOD NEWS GRAMMAR*

1 - Ser and Estar: to be and (not) to be

Unless you are a genius you are bound to get these two mixed up at times. But with *INSTANT Spanish* everybody will still understand you perfectly. Here are the main differences between **ser** and **estar** which both mean **(to) be**.

You use **ser** when you talk about something which is a basic characteristic of somebody or something and which does not change.

My name is Paco   Mi nombre **es** Paco. **Soy** Paco.
We are English   **Somos** ingleses

You also use **ser** for telling the time: ¿Qué hora **es**? Son las **tres**.

You use **estar** when you talk about something that is temporary, that can change.

The tables are not clean   Las mesas no **están** limpias. La ducha **está** rota.

You also use **estar** when someone or something is in a place, even if it is permanent!

Estamos en España. Londres **está** en Inglaterra. ¿Dónde **está**? **Estoy** aquí cerca.

And if you confuse them?… Don't worry. It's not *that* serious!
Here is a combined verb box. Spend five minutes on it.

ser		estar
soy … Juan	*I am*	**estoy – en Madrid**
es	*you are*	**está**
es	*he/she/it is*	**está**
es	*he/she/it is*	**está**
somos	*we are*	**estamos**
son	*they are*	**están**
son	*you are*	**están**

Remember, you and … you: use **es** and **está** when you talk to one person. Use **son** and **están** when you talk to two people or more.

2 - Saying not

If you want to say in Spanish that you are *not* doing something, you just add **no**. But did you notice what happened to the **no** when

Señora López said: '**No** es muy grande' and '**No** tomamos tarjetas' The **not** moved in front of the verb. It does this all the time; '…**not** is very big' '…**not** we take credit cards.'

*The table is **not** clean.*   La mesa **no** está limpia.
I do not work.   **No** trabajo.

No, no trabajo. Don't let this confuse you. The first **no** means *no*, the second one *not*.

3 - hay   there is/is there? - there are/are there?

You will use this a lot, especially when asking questions.

¿**Hay** un banco aquí cerca? ¿**Hay** un bar? ¿**Hay** servicios?
¿**Hay** un camarero guapo? ¡Sí, **hay** dos!

4 - Telling the time

las siete **menos cuarto**	**quarter to** seven
las diez **y cuarto**	**quarter past** ten
las dos **y media**	**half past** two
la una **y media**	**half past** one

❤️ 📼 LEARN BY HEART

Learn the six lines **No tengo mucho dinero, pero…** by heart.
When you know them try to say them fluently and fairly fast. How about 45 to 60 seconds?

Choose one of these to fill in the gaps:
   mi marido, mi mujer, mi amigo (boy/male friend), **mi amiga**

No tengo mucho dinero, pero…

No tengo mucho dinero pero quisiera ir de vacaciones en julio.
Quisiera ir a la Costa del Sol con.. .
Podemos ir a Marbella en el Rover.
No cuesta mucho y la Costa es muy bonita.
¿Podemos ir? ¡No!
Hay siempre mucho trabajo en la empresa y … ¡el Rover está roto!

Once again, give this piece some *life* when you know it by heart. Bits of it will come in handy later!

○ ◘ LET'S SPEAK SPANISH!

Now let's practise what you have learned. I give you 10 English sentences and you say them in Spanish – ALOUD! If you don't have the cassette, cover up the answers. Tick each sentence to check if you got it right. Unless you got all 10 correct, do the exercise again.

1 Do you have a room?
2 It is a little big.
3 At what time is the breakfast?
4 The computers are expensive.
5 We would like to eat something.
6 How much is (costs) the tea?
7 Where is the café, on the right?
8 We are going to Malaga at 2.
9 Excuse me, the bill, please.
10 Is there a bank near here?

*Now answer the questions on the left with **sí** and speak about yourself, and those on the right with **no** and say **we**.*

11 ¿Tiene una tarjeta Visa?
12 ¿Hay un bar aquí?
13 ¿Es una cuenta muy grande?

14 ¿Están de vacaciones?
15 ¿Trabajan ustedes diez horas?
16 ¿Tienen mucho dinero?

Now think up your own answers. Yours may be different from mine but quite correct.

17 ¿A qué hora va usted a Barcelona?
18 ¿Qué tal las tostadas?
19 ¿Dónde está la "Casa Margarita?"
20 ¿Hay servicios aquí? ¿Y dónde están?

ANSWERS

1 ¿Tiene (usted) una habitación?
2 Es un poco grande.
3 ¿A qué hora es el desayuno?
4 Los ordenadores son caros.
5 Quisiéramos comer algo.
6 ¿Cuánto cuesta el té?
7 ¿Dónde está la cafetería? ¿A la derecha?
8 Vamos a Málaga a las dos.
9 Perdone, la cuenta, por favor.
10 ¿Hay un banco aquí cerca?

11 Sí, tengo una tarjeta Visa.
12 Sí, hay un bar aquí.
13 Sí, es una cuenta muy grande.
14 No, no estamos de vacaciones.
15 No, no trabajamos diez horas.
16 No, no tenemos mucho dinero.
17 Voy a Barcelona a las tres y media.
18 Las tostadas están buenas, pero frías.
19 La "Casa Margarita" está en Sierra Nevada.
20 Sí, hay servicios aquí. Están todo recto.

If you managed to get more than half right the first time, give yourself a double gold star!

☑☒ TEST YOUR PROGRESS

Translate these sentences into Spanish and write them out.
See what you can remember without looking at the previous pages.

1 Where is there a telephone? On the right?
2 Can we eat some toast here? Are there seats for four?
3 Do you have a table? At half past eight? We are six.
4 Let's go to the bank and then to the cafeteria, all right?
5 Can you repair the Seat? It is broken.
6 We are in the room. Where are you?
7 The tapas are excellent. I can eat lots.
8 Can I ask you? You have a small company. Is it in Texas?
9 We cannot go on holiday in July. We do not have money.
10 Where is the waiter? Does he have my bill?
11 Where are the toilets? On the left?
12 Maria and I would like to go to Granada – without husbands.
13 Excuse me, I have only 5,000 pesetas and a credit card.
14 600 pesetas for a cold tortilla? It is very expensive.
15 I have been in Seville for one night. It costs less in November.
16 Mrs Lopez is very good-looking. Where does she work? Very near?
17 Agreed! We take the Seat for April.
18 London is not pretty in November.
19 I have worked a little with computers. It is not easy.
20 How many months have we been here? Fourteen?

Check your answers on page 61 and remember the scoring instructions.
Then enter your result on the Progress Chart.

Another 80% …?

3 | WEEK THREE DAY-BY-DAY GUIDE

Study for 35 minutes a day – but there are no penalties for more!

Day One
- Read LET'S GO SHOPPING.
- Listen to/Read VAMOS DE COMPRAS.
- Listen to/Read the NEW WORDS, then learn some of them.

Day Two
- Repeat VAMOS DE COMPRAS and NEW WORDS.
- Learn ALL NEW WORDS. Use the FLASH CARDS!

Day Three
- Test yourself on all NEW WORDS.
  Boring, boring, but you are over halfway already!
- Listen to/Read SPOT THE KEYS.
- Read GOOD NEWS GRAMMAR.

Day Four
- Go over GOOD NEWS GRAMMAR
- Cut out and learn the 10 FLASH SENTENCES.

Day Five
- Listen to/Read LET'S SPEAK SPANISH.
- Listen to/Read LEARN BY HEART.

Day Six
- Go over LEARN BY HEART.
- Have a quick look at NEW WORDS Weeks 1–3.
  You know 226 words by now! Well, more or less.
- Translate TEST YOUR PROGRESS.

Day Seven
Enjoy your day off!

🔊 LET'S GO SHOPPING

Tom and Kate have rented a holiday appartment just outside Marbella.
Kate plans to do some shopping.

Kate   Well, today we must go shopping. Are we going to the (town) centre?

Tom   But it makes bad weather. It makes cold and there is football and tennis in the television… and golf at twelve and half…

Kate   I am sorry but first we must go to a cash dispenser and to a tobacconist or to the post office to buy stamps…and then to the chemist's and the dry cleaner's.

Tom   And so there is no golf…. perhaps football at three o'clock… Is that all?

Kate   No, we must go to El Corte Inglés to buy a suitcase new and I must go to a supermarket and to the hairdresser. And then I would like to buy some shoes.

Tom   Good grief! (Mother of mine.) Until what hour are open the shops?

Kate   I believe (that) until 8 o'clock.

Tom   And so there is no football… perhaps tennis at eight and quarter.

(Later)

Kate   I believe that I have bought too much; a quarter of a kilo of ham, half kilo of cheese, 200 g of pâté, eggs, bread, butter, sugar, six beers and a bottle of wine dyed (red).

Tom   No problem. There is enough for two days. Not we have eaten anything since yesterday. And what is there in the bag big? Something for me?

Kate   Well, I have gone to the hairdresser of El Corte Inglés and afterwards I have seen some shoes in blue. They are great, aren't they? The sales assistant was very nice and handsome like Tom Cruise.

Tom   Who is Tom Cruise? And how much cost the shoes?

Kate   They were a little expensive… 24,000 pesetas… It is the same price in England!

Tom   What? My wife is mad!

Kate   But this T-shirt of golf was very cheap, size 50, only 2,000 pesetas, and here I have a newspaper English and not is there now tennis in the television?

🔊 📼 VAMOS DE COMPRAS

Tom and Kate have rented a holiday appartment just outside Marbella.
Kate plans to do some shopping.

Kate   Pues… hoy tenemos que ir de compras. ¿Vamos al centro?

Tom   Pero hace mal tiempo. Hace frío, y hay fútbol y tenis en la tele… y golf a las doce y media…

Kate   Lo siento, pero primero tenemos que ir a un cajero, y a un estanco o a correos para comprar sellos… y después a la farmacia y a la tintorería.

Tom   Entonces, no hay golf… quizás fútbol a las tres… ¿Es eso todo?

Kate   No, tenemos que ir a El Corte Inglés a comprar una maleta nueva, y yo tengo que ir a un supermercado y a la peluquería. Y luego quisiera comprar unos zapatos.

Tom   ¡Madre mía! ¿Hasta qué hora están abiertas las tiendas?

Kate   Creo que hasta las ocho.

Tom   Entonces, no hay fútbol… quizás tenis a las ocho y cuarto…

(Más tarde)

Kate   Creo que he comprado demasiado: un cuarto de kilo de jamón, medio kilo de queso, 200 gramos de paté, huevos, pan, mantequilla, azúcar, seis cervezas y una botella de vino tinto.

Tom   No importa. Hay bastante para dos días. No hemos comido nada desde ayer. Y ¿qué hay en la bolsa grande? ¿Algo para mí?

Kate   Pues, he ido a la peluquería del Corte Inglés y después he visto unos zapatos en azul. Son estupendos ¿verdad? El dependiente era muy amable y guapo, como Tom Cruise.

Tom   ¿Quién es Tom Cruise? Y ¿cuánto cuestan los zapatos?

Kate   Eran un poco caros… 24,000 pesetas… ¡Es el mismo precio en Inglaterra!

Tom   ¿Qué? ¡Mi mujer está loca!

Kate   Pero esta camiseta de golf era muy barata, talla 50, sólo 2,000 pesetas, y aquí tengo un periódico inglés y ¿no hay ahora tenis en la tele?

abcd... 🔊 NEW WORDS

Learn the new words in half the time by using FLASH CARDS.
There are 18 to start you off. Get a friend to make the rest!

hoy *today*
tenemos que *we have to, we must*
ir de compras *go shopping*
al centro *to the centre*
hace mal tiempo *it is bad weather* (lit. it makes…)
hace frío *it is cold* (it makes cold)
el fútbol *the football*
la tele, la televisión *the TV*
lo siento *I'm sorry*
primero *first*
un cajero *a cash dispenser*
el estanco *the tobacconist*
correos *the post office*
comprar *(to) buy*
los sellos *the stamps*
después *afterwards, then*
la farmacia *the chemist's*
la tintorería *the dry cleaner's*
entonces *and so*
quizás *perhaps*
ese, esa/eso (by itself) *that*
todo *all*
El Corte Inglés (a Spanish chain of department stores)
una maleta *suitcase*
nuevo/a *new*
tengo que *I have to, must*
un supermercado *a supermarket*
la peluquería *the hairdresser*
quisiera *I would like (to)*
los zapatos *the shoes*
¡Madre mía! *good grief!*
hasta *until*
abierto *open*

la tienda *the shop*
creo *I believe*
que *that*
más *more*
más tarde *later*
he comprado *I have bought, I bought*
demasiado *too, too much*
el jamón *the ham*
el queso *the cheese*
un gramo *a gram*
los huevos *the eggs*
el pan *the bread*
la mantequilla *the butter*
el azúcar *the sugar*
la cerveza *the beer*
una botella *a bottle*
el vino tinto *the red wine*
no importa *no problem*
bastante *enough, rather*
hemos comido *we have eaten*
nada *nothing*
desde *since*
ayer *yesterday*
la bolsa / el bolso *the bag / the handbag*
para mí *for me*
he ido *I have gone*
he visto *I have seen*
azul *blue*
¿verdad? *isn't it, aren't they, don't you, etc.*
el dependiente *the sales assistant*
era *he, she, it was, I was*
amable *kind, charming*
como *like*
quién *who*

eran *they were*
el mismo *the same*
el precio *the price*
Inglaterra *England*
loco/a *crazy*
este, esta / esto (by itself) *this*

la camiseta *the T-shirt*
barato *cheap*
la talla *the size*
un periódico *a newspaper*
inglés *English*

> **TOTAL NEW WORDS: 78**
> **...only 164 words to go!**

Some easy extras

Los colores (colours)

blanco *white*
negro *black*
rojo *red*
azul *blue*
verde *green*

amarillo *yellow*
marrón *brown*
gris *grey*
naranja *orange*
rosa *pink*

SPOT THE KEYS

By now you can say many things in Spanish. But what happens if you ask a question and do not understand the answer? Don't panic and go blank; just listen for the words you know. Any familiar words which you pick up will provide you with key words – clues to what the other person is saying. If you have the cassette, close the book now, listen to the dialogue and write down all the key words you have recognised.

Here's an example:

YOU Perdone, quisiera ir a correos. ¿Dónde está?

ANSWER Pues, *esmuysencillo: siga* **todo recto hasta** *el siguiente cruceconsemáforos. Hay algunosedificios, entreellos***una casa roja a la izquierda**. *Después hay una residenciadeancianos***y unas** *cuantas* **tiendas. A la derecha hay una tintorería**. *Atraviese***el parking y** *verálaoficina***de correos**.

With a lot of words running into each other you still managed to pick up: **todo recto – hasta – una casa roja – a la izquierda – unas tiendas – a la derecha – tintorería – el parking – de correos**. I think you'll get there.

☞ *GOOD NEWS GRAMMAR*

1 - The past

Imagine you are getting married today. You would say 'I do.' If it happened yesterday you would say 'I did' or 'I have done it.' When you want to talk about the past in Spanish the easiest way is to use **haber**, another kind of *have* (never **tener**!) plus a changed main verb. For example **trabajar** becomes **trabajado** and **comprar** becomes **comprado**. Let's put it together.

I bought, or I have bought	**he** comprado
You bought, or you have bought	**ha** comprado
He/she/it bought, or has bought	**ha** comprado
We bought, or we have bought	**hemos** comprado
They bought, or they have bought	**han** comprado
You (plural) bought, or have bought	**han** comprado

Not all *INSTANT* verbs are so well behaved and just change to **-ado**. Here are three odd ones which you'll use all the time.

ir	but:	**he ido**	*I went, I have gone*
ver	but:	**he visto**	*I saw, I have seen*
tener	but:	**he tenido**	*I had, I have had*

If you get confused there's a complete list of all *INSTANT* verbs in Week 6. Have a sneak preview. You know lots already!

2 - a + el = al and de + el = del

a and **de** plus **el** are always contracted to **al** and **del**.

Vamos **al** centro. Cinco minutos **del** bar.

3 - Tener que: 'must', 'have to'

How often do you say *I have to* or *I must*?
Tengo que trabajar. Tenemos que comprar… ¿Tiene que ir?
Don't forget the **que**!

4 - ir and poder: 'go' and 'can'

You know the routine. Say **ir** and **poder** with your eyes closed.

	I	*you/he/she/it*	*we*	*they/you*
ir:	**voy**	**va**	**vamos**	**van**
poder:	**puedo**	**puede**	**podemos**	**pueden**

◯ 💿 LET'S SPEAK SPANISH

If you have the cassette, close the book now. If not, cover up the answers below. Say one at a time – ALOUD.

1 I am sorry, I have to go.
2 We would like to go shopping.
3 Where are there shops?
4 At what time are they open?
5 I would like to buy bread.
6 Today it is very cold.
7 Good grief! Did you see it?
8 We have to buy milk.
9 We have eaten at (in) El Corte Inglés.
10 You don't have a TV? It doesn't matter.

*Answer these questions using the **I** form and the words in brackets.*

11 ¿Qué ha comprado? (un periódico inglés)
12 ¿Dónde ha comprado esto? (en el supermercado)
13 ¿Qué ha visto? (muchas tiendas)
14 ¿Qué ha comido? (una paella)
15 ¿Cuántas horas ha trabajado? (ocho horas)

*Now answer these questions with **no** and the **we** form of the verb.*

16 ¿Han ido al fútbol?
17 ¿Han comprado la tele?
18 ¿Tienen que ir a correos?
19 ¿Van al centro?
20 Finally, make up a giant sentence without drawing breath using **ahora – centro – Seat – mi amiga – tienda – comprar – zapatos – mi marido**. Start with: **Ahora ...**

---

1 Lo siento, tengo que ir.
2 Quisiéramos ir de compras.
3 ¿Dónde hay tiendas?
4 ¿A qué hora están abiertas?
5 Quisiera comprar pan.
6 Hoy hace mucho frío.
7 ¡Madre mía! ¿Lo ha visto?
8 Tenemos que comprar leche.
9 Hemos comido en El Corte Inglés.
10 ¿No tiene una tele? No importa.

11 He comprado un periódico inglés.
12 He comprado esto en el supermercado. *or* Lo he comprado...
13 He visto muchas tiendas
14 He comido una paella.
15 He trabajado ocho horas.
16 No, no hemos ido al fútbol.
17 No, no hemos comprado la tele.
18 No, no tenemos que ir a correos.
19 No, no vamos al centro.
20 Ahora voy al centro en el Seat con mi amiga a comprar zapatos a las tiendas para mi marido.

💛 📼 LEARN BY HEART

Try to say this dialogue in under one minute!

Vamos de compras

A   Hoy tenemos que ir de compras – vamos al centro.

B   Pero hace frío...

A   ¡No importa!

B   ¡Madre mía! ¡No tengo dinero! ¿Dónde hay un cajero?

A   Creo que he comprado demasiado: pan, mantequilla, jamón y queso... y seis botellas de vino blanco.

B   ¿Y las cervezas?

A   Ah... ¡lo siento!

The more expression you use when saying it, the easier it will be to remember it.

☑☒ TEST YOUR PROGRESS

Translate in writing. Then check the answers and be amazed!

1   We can buy stamps at (in) the tobacconist's, can't we?
2   Did you see the tennis on (in) the TV? Yes, I have seen everything.
3   She was very kind, like always.
4   Good grief! All the eggs are broken! It doesn't matter.
5   Yesterday was a rather good day.
6   The English newspapers were not cheap.
7   I believe that I have seen a dry cleaner in El Corte Inglés.
8   Until what time do you have to work? Until eight?
9   When do we have to go? I cannot go until later.
10 In November it is always bad weather in Manchester.
11 What did you buy? Six bottles of red wine? Great!
12 Size 44: what is that in English? Perhaps 14.
13 It is very cold in this house. I must buy something.
14 First I went shopping and then we ate with friends.
15 We have had the new TV since yesterday. And today it is broken.
16 You have bought a black case, not red, haven't you?
17 Everything was very expensive. So then we did not buy anything.
18 Who is the sales assistant? Where is there milk?
19 We do not have the T-shirt in green and at the same price.
20 I would like to buy something for me. But not too expensive.

Remember the Progress Chart. You are now halfway home!

4 | WEEK FOUR
DAY-BY-DAY GUIDE

Study 35 minutes a day but if you are keen try 40… 45…!

Day One
- Read LET'S GO AND EAT.
- Listen to/Read VAMOS A COMER.
- Listen to/Read NEW WORDS. Learn the easy ones.

Day Two
- Repeat the dialogue. Learn the harder NEW WORDS.
- Cut out the FLASH WORDS to help you.

Day Three
- Learn all NEW WORDS until you know them well.
- Read and learn GOOD NEWS GRAMMAR.

Day Four
- Cut out and learn the FLASH SENTENCES.
- Listen to/Read LEARN BY HEART.

Day Five
- Read SAY IT SIMPLY.
- Listen to/Read LET'S SPEAK SPANISH.

Day Six
- Listen to/Read SPOT THE KEYS.
- Translate TEST YOUR PROGRESS.

Day Seven
Are you keeping your scores over 60%? In that case
… **have a good day off!**

⑥⑨ LET'S GO AND EAT

Tom and Kate are still in Marbella. Juan Gálvez invites them to dinner.

Kate Somebody from Madrid has telephoned. He didn't say why (for what). I don't have the number, because (it is that) I didn't have paper at that moment. A name like Gámez or Gálvez.

Tom Ah yes, Juan Gálvez, a good client of the company. I know him well. He is very nice. I have an appointment with him on Tuesday. This is for an important matter.

Tom *(On the phone)* Hello, good morning Mr Gálvez. This is Tom Walker... Yes, thank you ... yes, sure, that is possible... on Tuesday, next week... correct... that's all right... yes, very interesting... no, we have time... great... no, only some days... oh yes... when?... at nine... upstairs, at the exit... in front of the door. And so, until tonight, thank you very much, until later.

Kate What are we doing this evening?

Tom We are going to eat with Mr Gálvez, in the centre, behind the church. He says that the restaurant is new and very good. He is in Marbella for two days with Edith and Peter Palmer from our company.

Kate I know Edith Palmer. I do not like her. She is boring and very snobbish. She has a terrible dog. I believe that I am going to be sick on Tuesday. A cold with pains. The doctor must come.

Tom No, please! Mr Gálvez is an important client. One cannot do that.

(In the restaurant): Luis, the head waiter, explains the menu.

Luis The fish is not on the menu, and the dessert today is ice cream of the house.

Juan Mrs Walker, what do you like? Perhaps a soup and then fish or meat?

Kate Well...a steak with salad, please.

Edith Too much red meat is not good for you, Kate.

Juan Mr Walker? Do you like the lamb? And what would you like to drink?

⋯⋯➡ Page 36

🔊 📼 VAMOS A COMER

Tom and Kate are still in Marbella. Juan Gálvez invites them to dinner.

Kate Tom, alguien de Madrid ha llamado. No ha dicho para qué. No tengo el número, es que en ese momento no he tenido papel. Un nombre como Gámez o Gálvez.

Tom Ah, sí, Juan Gálvez, un buen cliente de la empresa. Lo conozco bien. Es muy amable. Tengo una cita con él el martes. Esto es para una cosa importante.

Tom: *(Al teléfono)* Hola, buenos días Señor Gálvez. Soy Tom Walker ... Sí, gracias ... sí, seguro, eso es posible... el martes, la semana que viene,... correcto... está bien... sí, muy interesante ... no, tenemos tiempo... estupendo.... no, sólo unos días... ah sí... ¿cuándo?... a las nueve... arriba, a la salida... delante de la puerta... Entonces, hasta esta noche, muchas gracias, hasta luego.

Kate ¿Qué hacemos esta noche?

Tom Vamos a comer con el Señor Gálvez, en el centro, detrás de la iglesia. Dice que el restaurante es nuevo y muy bueno. Está en Marbella durante dos días, con Edith y Peter Palmer de nuestra empresa.

Kate Conozco a Edith Palmer. Ella no me gusta. Es aburrida y muy snob. Tiene un perro terrible. Creo que el martes voy a estar enferma. Un resfriado y dolores. El doctor tiene que venir.

Tom ¡No, por favor! El Sr. Gálvez es un cliente importante. Eso no se puede hacer.

(En el restaurante) Luis, the head waiter, explains the menu.

Luis El pescado no está en el menú, y el postre hoy es helado de la casa.

Juan Señora Walker, ¿qué le gusta? Quizás una sopa y después ¿pescado o carne?

Kate Pues...un filete con ensalada, por favor.

Edith Demasiada carne roja no es bueno para usted.

Juan Sr. Walker, ¿Le gusta el cordero? ¿Y qué quiere usted para beber?

⋯⟶ Page 37

Tom   Right… lamb chops for me with chips and vegetables – but all without garlic – and a beer please.

Edith   Tom, garlic is very good for you. I like it very much.

Juan   And you, Mrs Palmer?

Edith   A little roast chicken and a glass of still water, please.

(Later)

Juan   Have we finished? Does anyone want dessert… fruit… a coffee? Nobody? Well then, the bill please.

Edith   Ah, Sr. Gálvez, could you help me, please? How do you say 'doggie bag' in Spanish? I would like a bag for my dog.

Kate   But Edith, the dog is in England!

abcd… 🔊 NEW WORDS

alguien   *someone*
ha llamado   *has called*
ha dicho   *has said*
es que…   *it is that, that's because…*
el papel   *the paper*
el nombre   *the name*
el cliente   *the client*
conozco (a)   *I know* (usually somebody)
bien   *well, all right*
una cita   *an appointment*
él   *he, him*
martes   *Tuesday*
una cosa   *a thing, a matter*
importante   *important*
gracias, muchas gracias   *thank you, thank you very much*
seguro   *sure, certainly*
posible   *possible*
la semana que viene   *next week* (the week that comes)
correcto   *correct*
interesante   *interesting*
tiempo   *time,* also: *weather*

arriba   *above, upstairs*
la salida   *the exit*
delante (de)   *in front of*
la puerta   *the door*
hacemos   *we do*
detrás (de)   *behind*
la iglesia   *the church*
dice   *he, she, it says/you say*
el restaurante   *the restaurant*
durante   *during*
nuestro   *our*
me gusta/no me gusta   *I like (it)/I do not like (it)*
snob   *snobbish*
un perro   *a dog*
terrible   *terrible*
enfermo   *sick*
un resfriado   *a cold*
el dolor   *the pain*
el doctor   *the doctor*
venir   *(to) come*
no se puede hacer   *one cannot do that*
el pescado   *the fish*
el menú   *the menu*

Tom Bueno, para mí chuletas de cordero con patatas fritas y verdura – pero todo sin ajo – y una cerveza, por favor.

Edith Tom, el ajo es muy bueno para usted. A mí me gusta mucho.

Juan ¿Y usted, Sra Palmer?

Edith Un poco de pollo asado, un vaso de agua sin gas, por favor.

(Más tarde)

Juan ¿Hemos terminado? ¿Alguien quiere un postre.. fruta...un café? ¿Nadie? Bueno, la cuenta, por favor.

Edith Ah, Sr Gálvez, ¿podría ayudarme, por favor? ¿Cómo se dice 'doggy bag' en español? Quisiera una bolsa para mi perro.

Kate Pero Edith, ¡el perro está en Inglaterra!

el postre *the dessert*	**el pollo asado** *the roast*
helado *ice cream*	chicken
le gusta *you like, do you like?*	**la fruta** *the fruit*
una sopa *a soup*	**un vaso** *a glass*
la carne *the meat*	**el agua** *the water*
un filete *a fillet steak*	**con/sin gas** *carbonated /*
una ensalada *a salad*	*non-carbonated*
el cordero *the lamb*	**terminado** *finished*
¿qué quiere? *what do you want?*	**nadie** *nobody*
beber *drink*	**¿podría ayudarme?** *could*
las chuletas *the chops*	*you help me?*
las patatas fritas *the chips*	**¿cómo…?** *how…?*
la verdura *the vegetables*	**¿cómo se dice en español?**
el ajo *the garlic*	*how does one say in Spanish…?*

**TOTAL NEW WORDS: 68
...only 96 words to go!**

Last easy extras

Los días de la semana (days of the week)

lunes *Monday*	**viernes** *Friday*
martes *Tuesday*	**sábado** *Saturday*
miércoles *Wednesday*	**domingo** *Sunday*
jueves *Thursday*	

GOOD NEWS GRAMMAR

1 - The future

There is an easy way to say something that is going to happen in the future. You don't use *shall* or *will* but simply: *going to* or *go to*.

We are going to buy bread   **Vamos a comprar pan.**

2 - Me gusta – no me gusta

I like – I don't like – do you like…? You'll use this a lot!
In Spanish **gusta** is a bit of a strange construction. Think of it as saying that **something pleases you**.

me gusta el vino	*I like the wine*
le gusta el Seat	*you like the Seat*
le gusta el pan	*he/she likes the bread*
nos gusta la casa	*we like the house*
les gusta la fruta	*they like the fruit*

If you do not like something simply add **no**.
No me gusta el vino, or **el vino no me gusta**   *I do not like the wine*.

When you like or do not like more than one thing use **gustan**.
Pedro y Paco me gustan mucho. No me gustan las vacaciones.

3 - Conozco a Edith   'I know Edith'

When a verb is followed by a direct object which is a *person* you have to slip in an **a**. **He visto a Pepe** *I have seen Pepe.*

4 - 'Usted' or 'tu'?

When talking to people use **usted** – or the verb form that goes with it. **Tú** is informal and familiar and needs extra grammar.

5 - 'Comer' and 'querer': last two 'gift boxes'

Five minutes each should do it!
Comer is a team player. Many verbs ending in **-er** have endings like him.
Querer is a rebel. But you'll need **quisiera…** every day.

comer: *(to eat)*		**querer:** *(to) wish, want*	
com**o**	*I eat*	**quisiera**	*I would like*
com**e**	*you eat*	**quisiera**	*you would like*
com**e**	*he, she, it eats*	**quisiera**	*he, she, it would like*
com**emos**	*we eat*	**quisiéramos**	*we would like*
com**en**	*they, you eat*	**quisieran**	*they, you would like*

6 - Some easy extras: numbers and more about time

los numeros

11	once	19	diecinueve	50	cincuenta
12	doce	20	veinte	60	sesenta
13	trece	21	veintiuno	70	setenta
14	catorce	22	veintidós	80	ochenta
15	quince	23	veintitrés	90	noventa
16	dieciséis	30	treinta	100	ciento (cien)
17	diecisiete	31	treinta y uno (etc)	200	doscientos
18	dieciocho	40	cuarenta	1,000	mil

¿qué hora es?

¿a qué hora?	*at what time?*	**a las cinco**	*at five o'clock*
es la una	*it is one o'clock*	**son las dos**	*it is two o'clock*
un minuto	*a minute*	**una hora**	*an hour*
un día	*a day*	**una semana**	*a week*
un mes	*a month*	**un año**	*a year*

💟 📼 LEARN BY HEART

Here is someone who is rather fed-up. Act it out in 45 seconds!

No me gusta...

A ¿Conoce* al Señor Gómez?
Es un buen cliente de la empresa. Tengo que ir a comer con él.
B ¿Ah sí?
A No me gusta. No es amable. Come mucho y bebe más.
B ¿Y cuándo?
A ¡Esta noche! Hay fútbol en la tele.
Quisiera tener un resfriado pero eso no se puede hacer.
…¡Siempre la empresa!
B ¡Lo siento!

*(¿Conoce? *do you know?*)

🔆 SAY IT SIMPLY

When people want to speak Spanish but don't dare, it's usually because they are trying to *translate* what they want to say from English into Spanish. And when they don't know some of the words they give up!

With *INSTANT Spanish* you work around the words you don't know with the words you do know!

Believe me, with 390 words you can say anything!
It may not always be very elegant, but you are communicating!

Here are two examples showing you how to say things in a simple way. Words that are not part of the *INSTANT* vocabulary have been **highlighted**.

You need to **change** your **flight** from Tuesday to Friday.

Saying it simply:

No podemos ir el martes, quisieramos ir el viernes.
or: **No es posible ir el martes, tenemos que ir el viernes.**

You want to get your **purse** and **mobile phone** from the coach which the driver has locked.

Saying it simply:

Lo siento, tengo que ir en el bus. Mi dinero y mi pequeño teléfono están en el bus.
or: **Tengo que tener mi dinero y mi teléfono.
Desgraciadamente todo está en el bus.**

🔆 SAY IT SIMPLY – in the past

Here are 8 essential verbs for when you want to talk about the past – simply.

estar	*to be*	**he estado**	*I was, I have been*
comer	*to eat*	**he comido**	*I ate, I have eaten*
venir	*to come*	**he venido**	*I came, I have come*
hacer	*to do*	**he hecho**	*I did, I have done*
decir	*to say*	**he dicho**	*I said, I have said*
dar	*to give*	**he dado**	*I gave, I have given*
saber	*to know*	**he sabido**	*I knew, I have known*
escribir	*to write*	**he escrito**	*I wrote, I have written*

◯ ⬚ LET'S SPEAK SPANISH

Here are ten sentences as a warm-up! Use the cassette if you have it.

1 I do not like the client.
2 Do we go with him?
3 What do you want, the meat or the fish?
4 Yes sure, I would like to come.
5 Do you have an appointment for me?
6 I like going to Mallorca.
7 Who has said that?
8 Has someone called?
9 I know a cheap restaurant.
10 Can you help me, please?

*Now pretend you are in Spain with friends who do not speak Spanish. They want you to ask people things and will want **you** to do it for them in Spanish. They will say: **Please ask him...***

11 if he knows Edith Palmer.
12 if he likes lamb.
13 what he wants to drink.
14 if he has time next week.
15 if he has dogs.

*On another occasion they will ask you to **tell** people things. They say: **Please tell her** ... If you don't know the odd word use your INSTANT words.*

16 the soup is very cold.
17 that I am a vegetarian.
18 that we are in a rush now.
19 that nobody has seen him.
20 that I cannot go tomorrow.

---

1 No me gusta el cliente.
2 ¿Vamos con él?
3 ¿Qué quiere, la carne o el pescado?
4 Sí, seguro, quisiera venir.
5 ¿Tiene una cita para mí?
6 Me gusta ir a Mallorca.
7 ¿Quién ha dicho eso?
8 ¿Ha llamado alguien?
9 Conozco un restaurante barato.
10 ¿Puede ayudarme, por favor?

11 ¿Conoce a Edith Palmer?
12 ¿Le gusta el cordero?
13 Qué quiere beber?
14 ¿Tiene tiempo la semana que viene?
15 ¿Tiene perros?
16 Lo siento, pero la sopa está muy fría.
17 Ella/Él no come carne.
18 No, lo siento, pero no tenemos tiempo ahora.
19 Nadie lo ha visto.
20 Él/Ella no puede ir mañana.

🔊 📼 SPOT THE KEYS

You practised listening for key words when you asked the way to the post office in Week 3. Now you are in a department store and you ask the sales assistant if the black shoes you liked are also available in size 39:

Perdone, ¿tiene estos zapatos tambien en número treinta y nueve?

She said **no** *then* **un momento, por favor** *and disappeared. When she came back this is what she said:*

Acabo de mirar en el almacén y he llamado a otra sucursal, pero tienen los **zapatos sólo en marrón**. *Pero sé por experiencia que esta marca* **siempre viene en tallas muy grandes** *y en mi opinión el* **número treinta y ocho** *sería* **bastante grande**.

Size 39 was only available in brown but size 38 might be big enough.

☑☒ TEST YOUR PROGRESS

1 What did he say? He said: For whom are the chips?
2 Can you come to our house? Next week?
3 She says that the exit of the shop is upstairs behind the bar.
4 Do you know that he has gone to England?
5 What do you want? It is that…I am sick and I cannot work.
6 Could you help me, please? Is there a doctor here?
7 Is he going to the appointment without shoes? One cannot do that.
8 I know Isabel Romero. She is a very interesting woman.
9 Nobody can drink 15 beers in one night. It is not possible.
10 I like (the) dessert very much. I would like the ice cream.
11 He knows that it is an important matter, but he has no time.
12 We have finished and now we must go to Valencia.
13 I eat a lot of salads. What do you eat?
14 How do you like the fish? Without garlic?
15 The name of this vegetable: how does one say in Spanish…?
16 There are no shops in front of the church or behind. What do we do?
17 The company called. A Mr Lopez said that it was an important matter.
18 I am sure they have carbonated water. They always have it.
19 He says that he has pains since yesterday. Do you believe it?
20 I have a cold. I cannot go to England today.

How are your 'shares' looking on the Progress Chart? Going up?

5 | WEEK FIVE
DAY-BY-DAY GUIDE

How about 15 minutes on the train, tube or bus, 10 minutes on the way home and 20 minutes before switching on the television…?

Day One
- Read ON THE MOVE.
- Listen to/Read DE ACÁ PARA ALLÁ.
- Listen to/Read NEW WORDS. Learn 15 or more.

Day Two
- Repeat DE ACÁ PARA ALLÁ and NEW WORDS.
- Cut out the FLASH WORDS and get stuck in.

Day Three
- Test yourself to perfection on all NEW WORDS.
- Read and learn GOOD NEWS GRAMMAR.

Day Four (the tough day)
- Cut out and learn the FLASH SENTENCES.
- Listen to/Read LEARN BY HEART.

Day Five
- Listen to/Read LET'S SPEAK SPANISH.
- Go over LEARN BY HEART.

Day Six
- Listen to/Read SPOT THE KEYS.
- Translate TEST YOUR PROGRESS.

Day Seven
**How is the Progress Chart looking? Great?… Great!
I bet you don't want a day off … but I insist!**

ON THE MOVE

Tom and Kate are now travelling through Castilla, by train, bus and hire car. They talk to María, the ticket clerk at the station, to Jim on the train and later to Pepe, the bus driver.

At the railway station

Tom Two tickets to Toledo, please.

María Thereandback?

Tom There and what? Speak more slowly please.

María There – and – back?

Tom Single, please. When is there a train for Toledo and on what platform?

María At a quarter to ten, on platform number six.

Kate Come on, Tom, there are two seats here in non-smoking. Oh, there is somebody here who smokes. Excuse me, this is for non-smokers. It is forbidden to smoke here.

Jim Sorry, I don't understand, I speak only English.

At the bus stop

Kate They say that the bus for Madrid is coming in about 20 minutes. Tom, please, here are my postcards and a letter. There is a letter-box down there. I am going to take some photos of the river. It is very lovely with the sun.

Tom Kate, come on, two buses are coming. The two are yellow. This one is full. Let's take the other one.
(In the bus) Two to Madrid, please.

Pepe This bus goes to Toledo.

Tom But we are in Toledo!

Pepe Yes, yes, but this bus goes only to the Toledo hospital.

In the car

Tom Here comes our car. It costs only 10,000 pesetas for three days. I am very pleased.

Kate I do not like the car. I believe that it is very cheap because it is very old. Let's hope we do not have problems...

Tom I am sorry, but the first car was too expensive, the second one too big, this one was the last.

⋯⟶ Page 46

📼 DE ACÁ PARA ALLÁ

Tom and Kate are now travelling through Castilla – by train, bus and hire car. They talk to María, the ticket clerk at the station, to Jim on the train and later to Pepe, the bus driver.

En la estación de ferrocarril

Tom Dos billetes para Toledo, por favor.

María ¿Idayvuelta?

Tom ¿Ida y qué? Hable más despacio, por favor.

María ¿Ida – y – vuelta?

Tom Sólo ida, por favor. ¿Cuándo hay un tren para Toledo y en qué vía?

María A las diez menos cuarto, en la vía número seis.

Kate Venga, Tom, hay dos asientos aquí en no fumadores. Oh, aquí hay alguien que fuma. Perdone, esto es para no fumadores. Está prohibido fumar aquí.

Jim Sorry, no comprendo. Hablo only English.

En la parada del autobús

Kate Dicen que el autobús para Madrid viene en unos veinte minutos. Tom, por favor, aquí están mis tarjetas y una carta. Allí abajo hay un buzón. Yo voy a hacer unas fotos del río. Está muy bonito con el sol.

Tom Kate, venga, vienen dos autobuses. Los dos son amarillos. Éste está lleno. Vamos a tomar el otro.
(En el autobús) Dos a Madrid, por favor.

Pepe Este autobús va a Toledo.

Tom ¡Pero estamos en Toledo!

Pepe Sí, sí, pero este autobús va sólo al hospital de Toledo.

En el coche

Tom Aquí viene nuestro coche. Cuesta solo 10,000 pesetas por tres días. Estoy muy contento.

Kate El coche no me gusta. Creo que es muy barato porque es muy viejo. Esperamos no tener problemas....

Tom Lo siento, pero el primer coche era demasiado caro, el segundo demasiado grande, éste era el último.

⸺➤ Page 47

(Later)

The map is not (here). Where is the motorway? On the left there is a petrol station and a stop for the underground and on the right there is a school. Come on!

Kate The main road is over there, (where) by the traffic light. If we go to the end of the street we arrive at the motorway. Perhaps some three kilometres. *(On the motorway)* Why does the car go very slowly? Do we have enough petrol? How many litres? Do we have oil? Is the engine hot? I believe the car "has had it." Where is the mobile? Where is the number of the garage? Where is my handbag?

Tom Kate, please, all this is giving me a headache! And here comes the rain. And why are the police driving behind us?

abcd... 📼 NEW WORDS

de acá para allá *from here to there, on the move*
la estación *the station*
el ferrocarril *the railway*
el billete *the ticket*
ida y vuelta *return ticket ('gone and returned')*
hable más despacio *speak more slowly*
el tren *the train*
la vía *the platform*
venga *come!, come on!*
no fumadores *non-smoking*
fuma *he/she/it smokes, you smoke*
prohibido *forbidden*
fumar *(to) smoke*
comprendo *I understand*
hablo *I speak*
la parada *the stop*
el autobús *the bus*
dicen *they say*

viene *he/she/it comes, you come*
las tarjetas *the postcards*
la carta *the letter*
allí *there*
abajo *below, downstairs*
el buzón *the letter box*
hacer *do, make*
la foto *the photo*
el río *the river*
el sol *the sun*
vienen *they come*
éste *this one*
lleno *full*
el otro, la otra *the other*
el hospital *the hospital*
el coche *the car*
contento *pleased*
porque *because*
viejo/a *old*
esperamos *we hope, let's hope*
el problema *the problem*

(Más tarde)

El mapa no está. ¿Dónde está la autovía? A la izquierda hay una gasolinera y una parada de metro, y a la derecha hay un colegio. ¡Venga!

Kate La carretera está allí, donde el semáforo. Si vamos hasta el final de la calle llegamos a la autovía. Quizás unos tres kilómetros. *(En la autovía)* ¿Por qué va el coche muy lento? ¿Tenemos suficiente gasolina? ¿Cuántos litros? ¿Tenemos aceite? ¿El motor está caliente? Creo que el coche está roto. ¿Dónde está el movil? ¿Dónde está el número del taller? ¿Dónde está mi bolso?

Tom Kate, por favor, todo esto me da dolor de cabeza. ¡Y aquí viene la lluvia! ¿Y por qué va la policía detrás de nosotros?

segundo/a *second*	**suficiente** *enough*
último/a *last*	**la gasolina** *the petrol*
el mapa *the map*	**el litro** *the litre*
la autovía *the motorway*	**el aceite** *the oil*
la gasolinera *the petrol station*	**el motor** *the motor*
el metro *the underground*	**caliente** *hot*
un colegio *a school, college*	**el (teléfono) móvil** *the mobile*
la carretera *the main road*	*(phone)*
el semáforo *the traffic light*	**el taller** *the mechanic*
si *if*	**me** *me*
el final *the end*	**da** *he/she/it gives, you give*
la calle *the street*	**el dolor de cabeza** *the*
llegamos *we arrive*	*headache*
el kilómetro *the kilometre*	**la lluvia** *the rain*
por qué *why...?*	**la policía** *the police*
lento/a *slow*	

**TOTAL NEW WORDS: 68
...only 28 words to go!**

GOOD NEWS GRAMMAR

1 - 'lo' and 'la': it - 'los' and 'las': them

If you want to refer to something or someone – el camarero, la cuenta, los servicios or las tortillas – in English you would say *it* or *them*.
In Spanish you use **lo** (for **el** words), **la**, **los** or **las**. **Tengo el coche.** *I have it.* **Lo tengo. Tengo la cuenta.** *I have it.* **La tengo!** *Easy!*
The **lo**, **la**, **los** or **las** always go **in front of** the first verb:
Mi marido la (la ducha) puede reparar. My husband *it* can repair.

2 - ¿por qué?...¡porque! (twins, but not identical...)

por qué means *why?* Think of it as 'for what?'
porque means *because*. Think of it as 'for that…'

3 - ¿qué?... que... (more twins, not identical)

Have you noticed that all the question words carry accents?
¿cuándo? ¿cuánto? ¿cómo? ¿dónde? ¿qué?
Some of these reappear without the accent to introduce the answer.
¿Cómo es Bombay? ¿Como Nueva York. *Like New York.*

4 - Pronouns: 'me, mí, le, lo, la, él, ella, nos, les, los, las, ellos, ellas...' and more

Learning these 'cold' is rather disagreeable. Pick them up from the stories or from the FLASH SENTENCES. It's easier that way.

LEARN BY HEART

Someone has pranged the car and someone else is getting suspicious…! Say these lines like a prize-winning play!

Vamos al tenis

A ¿Vamos al tenis? Tengo dos billetes de la empresa. Me gustan mucho los americanos. Vamos en autobús o quizás en el metro. Hay también un tren, todo el día.

B ¿El autobús, el metro, un tren? ¿Por qué? Hay algo que no me gusta. Tenemos un coche abajo en la calle.

A Pues…con la lluvia no he visto el semáforo. Pero no es mucho, sólo la puerta, ¡y el jefe* del taller era muy amable!

(*el jefe: *the boss*)

◯ ▣ LET'S SPEAK SPANISH

Here's your ten-point warm up: respond to the answers with a question, referring to the words in CAPITAL LETTERS.

Example PEDRO **está aquí.** **¿Quién está aquí?**

1 El móvil no está EN MI BOLSO.
2 LA AUTOVÍA está al final de la carretera.
3 Hay un autobús EN VEINTE MINUTOS.
4 MI MARIDO quisiera hablar con el Señor González.
5 Ida y vuelta a Madrid cuesta, 4,000 PESETAS.
6 La casa no me gusta PORQUE ES VIEJA.
7 Van a Inglaterra EN COCHE.
8 Habla inglés MUY LENTO.
9 NO, el sueldo no me gusta.
10 SÍ, he estado contento con el colegio.

While out shopping with a friend you are offered various items to buy. You'll take them all saying: 'Yes, we buy it' or 'Yes, we buy them'.

11 ¿...y la cerveza?   **14** ¿...y las camisetas?
12 ¿...y el periódico?   **15** ¿...y el Mercedes?
13 ¿...y los pollos?   **16** ¿...y mi casa?

Here are four things you want to refer to but you don't know what they are called in Spanish. Explain them using the words you do know.

17 a daily help   **19** a teacher
18 a kennel   **20** to be broke

---

1 ¿Dónde está el móvil?
2 ¿Qué está al final de la carretera?
3 ¿Cuándo hay un autobús?
4 ¿Quién quisiera hablar con Sr. Gonzáles?
5 ¿Cuánto cuesta a Madrid ida y vuelta?
6 ¿Por qué no le gusta la casa?
7 ¿En qué van a Inglaterra?
8 ¿Cómo habla inglés?
9 ¿Le gusta el sueldo?
10 ¿Ha estado contento con el colegio?
11 Sí, la compramos.
12 Sí, lo compramos.

13 Sí, los compramos.
14 Sí, las compramos.
15 ¡Sí, lo compramos!
16 ¡Sí, la compramos!
17 Una señora que ayuda con el trabajo en la casa.
18 Una casa para los perrros cuando estamos de vacaciones.
19 Una señora o un señor que trabaja con los niños en el colegio.
20 No tenemos dinero. ¡No tenemos una peseta!

🔊 📼 SPOT THE KEYS

This time you plan a trip in the country and wonder about the weather.
This is what you would ask:

YOU: Perdone, ¿sabe qué tiempo tenemos hoy?

ANSWER: **Pues, no estoy muy seguro**, *pero de acuerdo con la última previsión* **en la tele** *hay un sistema lento de bajas presiones que se está alejando hacia el norte y se espera que* **hoy el tiempo** *sea bastante* **caliente**, *es decir* **unos treinta** *grados, pero por la noche se espera algunas tormentas* **y lluvia**.

He isn't sure, but according to the TV, something slow is happening (?) and it will be warm tomorrow – 30°C – but something (?) and rain in the night.

☑☒ TEST YOUR PROGRESS

Translate into Spanish

1 I don't like this car, the other car was better.
2 How much does the ticket cost – one way only?
3 What did you say? Speak more slowly, please.
4 We hope to buy petrol cheaper (more cheap) in Spain.
5 It is forbidden to smoke in the underground.
6 Is this correct? A yellow letterbox? I did not know it.
7 Can I speak with the mechanic? We are (at) 30 km from Madrid.
8 What is slower: the train or the car on (in) the motorway?
9 He did not see the traffic light, and now they are in the hospital.
10 There is a chemist's on (in) the main road, at (in) the bus stop.
11 I would like two return tickets, non-smoking.
12 The problem with her is that she smokes too much.
13 He has come here, to the end of the platform.
14 There is a lot of rain in England. I am pleased to be in Spain.
15 They say that the river is five minutes from the station.
16 If he does not give me the money, I am going to the police.
17 This is the last petrol station. Do we have enough oil and water?
18 They come in July. I do not understand why Pedro comes later?
19 I speak with him now. I have a mobile.
20 He has not eaten anything because he has (a) headache.

If you know all your words you should score over 90%!

6 | WEEK SIX DAY-BY-DAY GUIDE

This is your last week! Need I say more?

Day One
- Read IN THE AIRPORT.
- Listen to/Read EN EL AEROPUERTO.
- Listen to/Read NEW WORDS. There are only 28!

Day Two
- Repeat EN EL AEROPUERTO. Learn all NEW WORDS.
- Work with the FLASH WORDS and FLASH SENTENCES.

Day Three
- Test yourself on the FLASH SENTENCES.
- Listen to/Read and learn ¡ADIÓS!

Day Four
- No more GOOD NEWS GRAMMAR! Have a look at the summary.
- Read SAY IT SIMPLY.

Day Five
- Listen to/Read SPOT THE KEYS.
- Listen to/Read LET'S SPEAK SPANISH.

Day Six
- Your last TEST YOUR PROGRESS! Go for it!

Day Seven

Congratulations!

You have successfully completed the course and can now speak

INSTANT Spanish!

IN THE AIRPORT

Tom and Kate are on their way home to Birmingham. They are in the departure lounge of Barcelona airport and meet an old friend...

Tom   We have to work on Monday. What a bore! I would like to go to Italy, or better, to Hawaii. My company can wait and nobody is going to know where I am.

Kate   And what are the people in _my_ company going to say? They are going to wait for two days and then they are going to phone my mother. She'll surely know the number of our mobile. And then?

Tom   Yes, yes, I know it. Well, perhaps a week's holiday at Christmas in the snow or on a boat to Madeira... I am going to buy a newspaper... Kate! Here is Pedro Iglesias!

Pedro   Well, hello! How are you! What are you doing here? This is my wife, Nancy. How were your holidays? Are they finished?

Kate   The holidays...? ...hmmm ... great! We know Andalucia and Castilla well now.

Pedro   Next year you must go to Santander or Pamplona. Mrs. Walker, my wife would like to buy a book about computers. Would you mind going with her and helping her, please? Mr. Walker, you have a newspaper. What is happening with the football? And ... would you like to have a drink?

(In a shop at the airport)

Kate   I don't see anything. There is nothing that I like. Are you also going to England?

Nancy   No, we are going to Madrid to (the house of) Pedro's mother. Our children are always there during the holidays. We have a boy and three girls. Tomorrow we are going to take the train. It is cheaper.

Kate   Your husband works for the Bank of Spain, doesn't he?

Nancy   Yes, his work is interesting but the pay is bad. We have a small appartment and an old car. We have to repair lots of things. My mother is in Los Angeles and I have a girl-friend in Dallas and we write a lot of letters. I would like to go to America but it costs too much money.

······➤ Page 54

👄 📼 EN EL AEROPUERTO

Tom and Kate are on their way home to Birmingham. They are in the departure lounge of Barcelona airport and meet an old friend ...

Tom   El lunes tenemos que trabajar. ¡Qué lata! Quisiera ir a Italia o mejor a Hawaii. Mi empresa puede esperar, y nadie va a saber dónde estoy.

Kate   ¿Y qué va a decir la gente en *mi* empresa? Van a esperar durante dos días y después van a llamar a mi madre. Seguro que ella sabe el número de nuestro móvil. ¿Y después?

Tom   Sí, sí, lo sé. Pues, quizás en Navidad una semana de vacaciones en la nieve o en barco a Madeira..... Voy a comprar el periódico......¡Kate! ¡Aquí está Pedro Iglesias!

Pedro   ¡Hombre! ¿Qué tal?¿Qué hacen aquí? Ésta es mi mujer, Nancy. ¿Qué tal las vacaciones, han terminado?

Kate   ¿Las vacaciones? ... hmmm ... ¡estupendas! Ahora conocemos bien Andalucía y Castilla.

Pedro   El año que viene tienen que ir a Santander o Pamplona. Señora Walker, mi mujer quisiera comprar un libro de ordenadores. ¿Le importaría ir con ella y ayudarla por favor? Señor Walker, Usted tiene un periódico. ¿Qué pasa con el fútbol? Y... ¿quiere tomar una copa?

(En una tienda del aeropuerto)

Kate   No veo nada. No hay nada que me gusta. ¿Va usted también a Inglaterra?

Nancy   No, vamos a Madrid a casa de la madre de Pedro. Nuestros niños siempre están allí durante las vacaciones. Tenemos un hijo y tres hijas. Mañana vamos a tomar el tren. Es más barato.

Kate   Su marido trabaja en el Banco de España, ¿verdad?

Nancy   Sí, su trabajo es interesante, pero el sueldo es malo. Tenemos un piso pequeño y un coche viejo. Tenemos que reparar muchas cosas. Mi madre está en Los Angeles y tengo una amiga en Dallas y nos escribimos muchas cartas. Quisiera ir a América pero cuesta demasiado dinero.

⸺➤ Page 55

54

Kate But you have a lovely house in Mallorca.

Nancy A house in Mallorca? I have never been in Mallorca. When we have holidays we go to (the house of) a friend in Bilbao.

Tom Kate, come on, we have to go to the plane. Goodbye!.... What is the matter Kate? What did Nancy say?

Kate Wait Tom, wait!!

abcd... 📼 NEW WORDS

el aeropuerto *the airport*

¡qué lata! *what a bore, nuisance!*

esperar *(to) wait*

saber *(to) know*

decir *(to) say*

la gente *the people*

llamar *(to) call*

la madre *the mother*

sé *I know*

en Navidad *at Christmas*

la nieve *the snow*

el barco *the ship, boat*

¡hombre! *well, hello!* (surprise greeting)

hacen *they do, you do*

conocemos *we know*

el libro *the book*

¿Le importaría? *would you mind?*

¿qué pasa? *what is happening? what is the matter?*

una copa *a drink*

veo *I see*

el hijo (m) *the son, child* (m)

la hija *the daughter, child* (f)

el piso *the appartment, flat*

vive *he/she/it lives, you live*

nos *us*

escribimos *we write*

nunca *never*

espera / espere *wait!* (friendly), *wait* (formal)

TOTAL NEW WORDS: 28
TOTAL SPANISH WORDS LEARNED: 390
EXTRA WORDS: 68

GRAND TOTAL: 458

Kate   Pero usted tiene una casa bonita en Mallorca.

Nancy   ¿Una casa en Mallorca? No he estado nunca en Mallorca. Cuando tenemos vacaciones vamos a la casa de un amigo en Bilbao.

Tom   Kate, venga, tenemos que ir al avión. ¡Adiós…! ¿Qué pasa Kate? ¿Qué ha dicho Nancy?

Kate   ¡Espera, Tom, espera…!

❤ 📼 *LEARN BY HEART*

This is your last dialogue to LEARN BY HEART. Give it your best! You now have six prize-winning party pieces, and a large store of everyday sayings which will be very useful.

¡Adiós…!

Kate Señor Gálvez, buenos días, soy Kate Walker.
Llamo del aeropuerto.
Sí, la vacaciones han terminado y el dinero también, desgraciadamente.
Tom quisiera hablar con usted…y…¡adiós!

Tom ¡Hola, Juan! ¿Qué? ¿Cómo? ¿Compra los dos?
¿Mi empresa tiene su e-mail*? ¡Estupendo! ¡Muchas gracias!
¿El año que viene?
Kate quisiera ir a Italia, pero a mí me gusta España.
¿Con Edith Palmer? ¡POR FAVOR!
Tenemos que ir al avión…¡Adiós!

(*officially: correo electrónico)

📻 GOOD NEWS GRAMMAR

As promised there is no new grammar in this lesson, just a summary of all the 31 *INSTANT* verbs which appear in the six weeks. This is not for learning, just for a quick check. You know and have used most of them!

Basic form	I	You, he, she, it	We	They, you	The past
ayudar*	ayudo	ayuda	ayudamos	ayudan	ayudado
beber*	bebo	bebe	bebemos	beben	bebido
comer*	como	come	comemos	comen	comido
comprar*	compro	compra	compramos	compran	comprado
comprender*	comprendo	comprende	comprendemos	comprenden	comprendido
conocer	conozco	conoce	conocemos	conocen	conocido
creer*	creo	cree	creemos	creen	creido
costar		cuesta		cuestan	
dar	doy	da	damos	dan	dado
decir	digo	dice	decimos	dicen	dicho
escribir	escribo	escribe	escribimos	escriben	escrito
esperar*	espero	espera	esperamos	esperan	esperado
estar	estoy	está	estamos	están	estado
fumar*	fumo	fuma	fumamos	fuman	fumado
haber	he	ha	hemos	han	
hablar*	hablo	habla	hablamos	hablan	hablado
hacer	hago	hace	hacemos	hacen	hecho
ir	voy	va	vamos	van	ido
llamar*	llamo	llama	llamamos	llaman	llamado
llegar*	llego	llega	llegamos	llegan	llegado
poder	puedo	puede	podemos	pueden	podido
querer	quisiera	quisiera	quisiéramos	quisieran	
reparar*	reparo	repara	reparamos	reparan	reparado
saber	sé	sabe	sabemos	saben	sabido
ser	soy	es	somos	son	sido
tener	tengo	tiene	tenemos	tienen	tenido
tomar*	tomo	toma	tomamos	toman	tomado
trabajar*	trabajo	trabaja	trabajamos	trabajan	trabajado
venir	vengo	viene	venimos	vienen	venido
ver	veo	ve	vemos	ven	visto
vivir	vivo	vive	vivimos	viven	vivido

*member of the Good Verbs Team

 **SAY IT SIMPLY**

Here are two more exercises to practise using plain language:

1 You have just hired a car and notice a big scratch on the left, behind the door. You want to report it as not to get the bill for it later.

2 You are at the airport, about to catch your flight home when you realise that you have left some clothes behind in the room of your hotel. You phone the hotel's housekeeper to ask her to send the things on to you.

What would you say? Say it then write it down. Then see page 63.

SPOT THE KEYS

Here are two final practice rounds. If you have the cassette close the book NOW. Find the key words and try to get the gist of it. Then check on page 63.

1   This is what you might ask of a taxi driver:

YOU   **¿En cuánto tiempo se llega* al aeropuerto y cuánto cuesta?**

ANSWER   *Depende de la hora en que vaya a salir. Normalmente se llega en unos veinte minutos, pero si viajamos en hora punta y hay mucho tráfico y si hay atascos sobre el puente del río debe calcular unos cuarenta y cinco minutos. El precio se indica en el taxímetro. Normalmente cuesta entre 4.000 y 5.000 pesetas.*

(*in how much time does one arrive = how long does it take)

2   While killing time in the departure lounge of the airport you could not help listening to someone who seems to be raving about something. Identify keys and guess where they have been. The answer is on page 63.

…y mi marido dijo también que le había gustado mucho más que nuestras vacaciones aquí. Y la gente era muy amable y no tan reservada como siempre dicen. Y el hotel estaba directamente sobre el lago, con unas habitaciones muy bonitas y hacía un tiempo estupendo y paseamos muchísimo y también fuimos de excursión con el coche y vimos tantas cosas interesantes. Y entonces decidimos sin más que el año que viene vamos a volver a…

♀ ⏭ *LET'S SPEAK SPANISH*

Here's a five-point warm up: answer these questions using the words in brackets.

1 ¿Ha comprado el piso en Marbella? (Sí, lo, lunes)
2 ¿Cuántos años ha trabajado allí? (durante tres)
3 ¿Cuándo ha hablado con la empresa? (con ella, esta semana)
4 ¿Por qué tiene que reparar su coche? (mi coche, porque es viejo)
5 ¿Ha ido primero con su madre? (no, con el cliente)

In your last exercise you are going to interpret again, this time telling your Spanish friend what others have said in English. Each time say the whole sentence ALOUD, translating the English words.

6 Alguien ha dicho, que está loco (if you buy this old flat).
7 Alguien ha dicho que no le gusta (if we eat too late).
8 Ha dicho que algo está roto (if you have no hot water).
9 Mi amiga ha dicho (that our holiday is over).
10 Ha dicho también (that next year we go to America).
11 Mi mujer quisiera decir (that she has a cold).
12 Mi marido dice que no puede venir (because he works on a ship).
13 No puede venir en Navidad (because his friend is coming).
14 Mi amigo dice (that you are very good-looking).
15 También dice (that he would like your mobile number).

---

1 Sí, lo ha comprado el lunes.
2 He trabajado allí durante tres años.
3 He hablado con ella esta semana.
4 Tengo que reparar mi coche porque es muy viejo.
5 No, primero ha ido con el cliente.
6 ...si compra este piso viejo.
7 ...si comemos demasiado tarde.
8 ...si no tiene agua caliente.
9 ...que nuestras vacaciones han terminado.
10 ...que el año que viene vamos a America.
11 ...que tiene un resfriado.
12 ...porque trabaja en un barco.
13 ...porque viene su amigo.
14 ...que usted es muy guapa.
15 ...que quisiera su número móvil.

Now do it once more – FAST!

☑☒ TEST YOUR PROGRESS

A lot has been crammed into this last test – all 31 *INSTANT* verbs!
But don't panic – it looks worse than it is. Go for it – you'll do
brilliantly!

Translate into Spanish:

1   I like writing letters because I have a new computer.
2   How are you? What is the matter? Can I help you?
3   The people in the company are rather boring.
4   I do not have the number of her mobile, I am sorry.
5   Do you like the Sierra Nevada? We had a lot of snow this year.
6   The second case is in the bus. Did you see the black bag?
7   How many cards did you write (at) (in) Christmas? Eighty-eight?
8   That's terrible. They have not eaten for five days.
9   Why did you not telephone? We waited since yesterday.
10 When we arrive we'll have (take) a drink – or two.
11 Don't you know that? The airport is always open – day and night.
12 We are sure that he has done it.
13 We have worked (for) many years but never on a boat.
14 I have given my car to my son. He is very pleased.
15 Your mother is very nice and makes great paella.
16 Do you live in a house or a flat in Torremolinos?
17 We must work many hours. Four daughters cost a lot of money.
18 Can the mechanic repair that? I think so.
19 I know him. He always goes shopping with his dog.
20 Who said one cannot smoke here?
21 We go by plane to Dallas. Then we go by car to Las Vegas.
22 I would like to speak with the sales assistant. He did not give me
    the bill.
23 We drank your wine but we have come today with two more bottles.
24 I am sorry, but *INSTANT Spanish* is now finished.

Check your answers on page 63. Then enter a final excellent score
on the Progress Chart and – write out your Certificate!

60

🔑 ANSWERS

How to score

From a total of 100%
- Subtract 1% for each wrong or missing word.
- Subtract 1% for the wrong form of the verb. Example *we have* **tengo (tenemos)**.
- Subtract 1% every time you mixed up the present and the past tenses.

There are no penalties for:
- wrong use all those little words, like: **el, la/un, una/a el (al)**, etc.
- wrong ending of adjectives like: **un coche barata (barato)**
- wrong use of **ser** and **estar**
- wrong choice of words with similar meaning like: **en** and **a**
- wrong or different word order
- wrong spelling or missing accents – as long as you can *say* the word: **qué/que, quatro (cuatro), ora (hora), rotto (roto)**, etc.
- missing or incorrect punctuation like ¿ or ¡.

> **100% LESS YOUR PENALTIES WILL GIVE YOU YOUR WEEKLY SCORE**

WEEK 1
TEST YOUR PROGRESS

1 Me llamo Peter Smith.
2 ¡Hola, somos Helen y Pepe!
3 Soy de Toledo. ¿Y usted?
4 María es una buena amiga.
5 Siempre voy a casa en junio.
6 Trabajamos en Alicante en agosto.
7 ¿(Usted) Va siempre a Nueva York en marzo?
8 ¿En qué trabaja (usted)? ¿Trabaja (usted) con ordenadores?
9 Está en Londres con los niños.
10 Un momento por favor. ¿Qué es? ¿Cuesta mucho?
11 ¿La casa tiene teléfono? No, desgraciadamente, no.
12 Buenos días, ¿es usted la señora López de Madrid?
13 Trabajo sin sueldo en una empresa americana.
14 Ahora tengo un trabajo mejor. Trabajo para tres bancos grandes.
15 ¡Paco! ¿Qué tal? ¿Vamos a Sevilla?
16 Mi mujer también es americana. Es de Boston.
17 Tenemos buenos asientos en el avión.
18 ¿Yo tengo un Mercedes? ¡Qué va!
19 Mi amiga habla español, pero no mucho.
20 Voy de vacaciones con Carmen. Desgraciadamente es aburrida.

> **YOUR SCORE:** _____ %

Correct those answers which differ from yours. Then read them aloud twice.

WEEK 2
TEST YOUR PROGRESS

1 ¿Dónde hay un teléfono? ¿A la derecha?
2 ¿Podemos comer unas tostadas aquí? ¿Hay asientos para cuatro?
3 ¿Tiene una mesa? ¿A las ocho y media? Somos seis.
4 Vamos al banco y luego a la cafetería, ¿vale?
5 ¿Puede reparar el Seat? Está roto.
6 Estamos en la habitación ¿Dónde está (usted)?
7 Las tapas están estupendas. Puedo comer muchas.
8 ¿Puedo preguntarle? (Usted) Tiene una empresa pequeña. ¿Está en Texas?
9 No podemos ir de vacaciones en julio. No tenemos dinero.
10 ¿Dónde está el camarero? ¿Tiene mi cuenta?
11 ¿Dónde están los servicios? ¿A la izquierda?
12 María y yo quisiéramos ir a Granada – sin maridos.
13 Perdone, tengo sólo cinco mil pesetas y una tarjeta de crédito.
14 ¿Seiscientas pesetas para una tortilla fría? Es muy cara.
15 He estado en Sevilla para una noche. Cuesta menos en noviembre.
16 La Señora López es muy guapa. ¿Dónde trabaja? ¿Muy cerca?
17 ¡De acuerdo! Tomamos el Seat para abril.
18 Londres no es bonito en noviembre.
19 He trabajado un poco con ordenadores. No es fácil.
20 ¿Cuántos meses hemos estado aquí? ¿Catorce?

> **YOUR SCORE:** _____ %

WEEK 3
TEST YOUR PROGRESS

1 Podemos comprar sellos en los estancos, ¿verdad?
2 ¿Ha visto el tenis en la tele? Sí, he visto todo.
3 Era muy amable, como siempre.
4 ¡Madre mía! ¡Todos los huevos están rotos! No importa.
5 Ayer era un día bastante bueno.
6 Los periódicos ingleses no eran baratos.
7 Creo que he visto una tintorería en El Corte Inglés.
8 ¿Hasta qué hora tiene que trabajar? ¿Hasta las ocho?
9 ¿Cuándo tenemos que ir? No puedo ir hasta más tarde.
10 En noviembre siempre hace mal tiempo en Manchester.
11 ¿Qué ha comprado? ¿Seis botellas de vino tinto? ¡Estupendo!
12 Talla cuarenta y cuatro: ¿qué es eso en inglés? Quizás catorce.
13 Hace mucho frío en esta casa. Tengo que comprar algo.
14 Primero he ido de compras y después hemos comido con amigos.
15 Hemos tenido la nueva tele desde ayer. ¡Y hoy está rota!
16 Ha comprado una maleta negra, no roja ¿verdad?
17 Todo era muy caro. Entonces no hemos comprado nada.
18 ¿Quién es el dependiente? Dónde hay leche?
19 No tenemos la camiseta en verde y al mismo precio.
20 Quisiera comprar algo para mí. Pero nada demasiado caro.

> **YOUR SCORE:** _____ %

WEEK 4
TEST YOUR PROGRESS

1   ¿Qué ha dicho? Ha dicho: '¿Para quién son las patatas fritas?'
2   ¿Puede venir a nuestra casa? ¿La semana que viene?
3   Dice que la salida de la tienda está arriba, detrás del bar.
4   ¿Sabe que ha ido a Inglaterra?
5   ¿Qué quiere? Es que…estoy enfermo y no puedo trabajar.
6   ¿Podría ayudarme, por favor? ¿Hay un doctor aquí?
7   ¿Va a la cita sin zapatos? Esto no se puede hacer.
8   Conozco a Isabel Romero. Es una señora muy interesante.
9   Nadie puede beber quince cervezas en una noche. No es posible.
10   El postre me gusta mucho. Quisiera el helado.
11   Sabe que es una cosa importante pero no tiene tiempo.
12   Hemos terminado y ahora tenemos que ir a Valencia.
13   Como muchas ensaladas. ¿Qué come usted?
14   ¿Cómo le gusta el pescado? ¿Sin ajo?
15   El nombre de esta verdura: ¿cómo se dice … en español?
16   No hay tiendas delante de la iglesia o detrás. ¿Qué hacemos?
17   Ha llamado la empresa. Un Señor López ha dicho que es una cosa importante.
18   Estoy seguro que tienen agua con gas. Lo tienen siempre.
19   Dice que tiene dolores desde ayer. ¿Lo cree?
20   Tengo un resfriado. No puedo ir a Inglaterra hoy.

> YOUR SCORE: _____ %

WEEK 5
TEST YOUR PROGRESS

1   Este coche no me gusta. El otro coche era mejor.
2   ¿Cuánto es/cuesta el billete – sólo ida?
3   ¿Qué ha dicho? Hable más despacio, por favor.
4   Esperamos comprar la gasolina más barata en España.
5   Está prohibido fumar en el metro.
6   ¿Es esto correcto? ¿Un buzón amarillo? No lo he sabido.
7   ¿Puedo hablar con el taller? Estamos a treinta kilómetros de Madrid.
8   ¿Qué es más lento? ¿El tren o el coche en la autovía?
9   No ha visto el semáforo, y ahora están en el hospital.
10   Hay una farmacia en la carretera, en la parada del autobús.
11   Quisiera dos billetes ida y vuelta, no fumadores.
12   El problema con ella es que fuma demasiado.
13   Ha venido aquí, al final de la vía.
14   Hay mucha lluvia en Inglaterra. Estoy contento de estar en España.
15   Dicen que el río está a cinco minutos de la estación.
16   Si no me da el dinero voy a la policía.
17   Esta es la última gasolinera. ¿Tenemos suficiente agua y aceite?
18   Vienen en julio. No comprendo por qué Pedro viene más tarde.
19   Hablo con él ahora. Tengo un móvil.
20   No ha comido nada porque tiene dolor de cabeza.

> YOUR SCORE: _____ %

WEEK 6
TEST YOUR PROGRESS

1   Me gusta escribir cartas, porque tengo un nuevo ordenador.
2   ¿Qué tal? ¿Qué pasa? ¿Puedo ayudarle?
3   La gente en la empresa está bastante aburrida.
4   No tengo el número de su móvil, lo siento.
5   ¿Le gusta la Sierra Nevada? Este año hemos tenido mucha nieve.
6   La segunda maleta está en el autobús. ¿Ha visto el bolso negro?
7   ¿Cuántas tarjetas ha escrito en Navidad? ¿Ochenta y ocho?
8   Esto es terrible. No han comido durante cinco días.
9   ¿Por qué no ha llamado por teléfono? Hemos esperado desde ayer.
10 Cuando llegamos tomamos una copa – o dos.
11 ¿No lo sabe? El aeropuerto está abierto siempre – día y noche.
12 Estamos seguros que lo ha hecho.
13 Hemos trabajado muchos años pero nunca en un barco.
14 He dado mi coche a mi hijo. Está muy contento.
15 Su madre es muy amable y hace una paella estupenda.
16 ¿Vive usted en un piso o en una casa en Torremolinos?
17 Tenemos que trabajar muchas horas. Cuatro hijas cuestan mucho.
18 ¿Lo puede reparar el taller? Creo que sí.
19 Lo conozco. Siempre va de compras con su perro.
20 ¿Quién ha dicho que no se puede fumar aquí?
21 Vamos a Dallas en avión. Luego vamos a Las Vegas en coche.
22 Quisiera hablar con el dependiente. No me ha dado la cuenta.
23 Hemos bebido su vino pero hemos venido hoy con dos botellas más.
24 Lo siento, pero *INSTANT Spanish* ha terminado ahora.

> **YOUR SCORE:** _____ %

SAY IT SIMPLY

1 Perdone, hay un problema con el coche. ¿Puede venir, por favor? Esto, detrás de la puerta, aquí a la izquierda. Yo no lo he hecho. No quisiera tener un problema más tarde.

2 Hola, buenos días, soy Kate Walker. El número de mi habitación es el 32. Llamo del aeropuerto. Tengo unas cosas en la habitación y ahora vamos a Birmingham. Lo siento, pero ¿puede ayudarme por favor? Tengo que tener las cosas. El hotel sabe dónde vivo en Birmingham. Muchas gracias.

SPOT THE KEYS

1 It depends on the time you are going to leave. Normally it takes about 25 minutes but if we leave in the rush hour and there is a lot of traffic and a traffic-jam on the bridge over the river, you have to calculate some 45 or 50 minutes. The price is shown on the metre. Normally it costs between 4,000 and 5,000 pesetas.

2 They had of course been in England!

⚡HOW TO USE THE FLASH CARDS

The Flash cards have been voted the best part of this course! Learning words and sentences can be tedious but with flashcards it's quick and good fun.

This is what you do:

When the Day-by-Day Guide tells you to use the cards cut them out. There are 18 FLASH WORDS and 10 FLASH SENTENCES for each week. Each card has a little number on it telling you to which week it belongs, so you won't cut out too many cards at a time or muddle them up later on.

First try to learn the words and sentences by looking at both sides. Then, when you have a rough idea, start testing yourself – that's the fun bit. Look at the English, say the Spanish, and then check. Make a pile for the 'correct' and one for the 'wrong' and 'don't know'. When all cards are used up start again with the 'wrong' pile and try to whittle it down until you got all of them right. You can also play it 'backwards' by starting with the Spanish face-up.

Keep the cards in a little box or put an elastic band around them. Take them with you on the bus, the train, to the hairdresser or the dentist.

If you find the paper too flimsy photocopy the words and sentences onto card before cutting them up. You could also buy some plain card and stick them on or simply copy them out.

The 18 FLASH WORDS for each week are there to start you off. **Convert the rest of the NEW WORDS to FLASH WORDS, too.** It's well worth it!

FLASH CARDS for INSTANT LEARNING:
DON'T LOSE THEM – USE THEM!

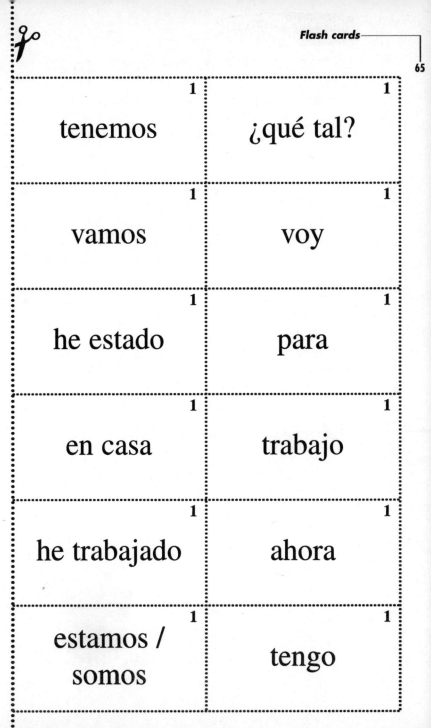

tenemos [1]	¿qué tal? [1]
vamos [1]	voy [1]
he estado [1]	para [1]
en casa [1]	trabajo [1]
he trabajado [1]	ahora [1]
estamos / somos [1]	tengo [1]

how are you? [1]	we have [1]
I go [1]	we go, we are going, let's go [1]
for [1]	I have been, I was [1]
I work [1]	at home [1]
now [1]	I have worked [1]
I have [1]	we are [1]

1 tiene	1 siempre
1 está / es	1 también
1 de vacaciones	1 desgraciadamente
2 a la derecha	2 a la izquierda
2 algo	2 caro / cara
2 cerca	2 comer

always [1]	he, she, it has / you have [1]
also [1]	he, she, it is, you are [1]
unfortunately [1]	on holiday [1]
on the left [2]	on the right [2]
expensive [2]	something [2]
(to) eat [2]	near [2]

2 cuánto…?	2 dónde…?
2 el desayuno	2 estupendo/a
2 hay	2 ir
2 la cuenta	2 luego
2 muy	2 puedo
2 podemos	2 quisiéramos

where? **2**	how much…? **2**
great **2**	the breakfast **2**
(to) go **2**	there is **2**
then, afterwards **2**	the bill **2**
I can **2**	very **2**
we would like (to) **2**	we can **2**

primero **3**	un cajero **3**
el estanco **3**	correos **3**
comprar **3**	los sellos **3**
después **3**	quizás **3**
quisiera **3**	tengo que **3**
hasta **3**	abierto/a **3**

a cash dispenser [3]	first [3]
the post office [3]	the tobacconist's [3]
the stamps [3]	(to) buy [3]
perhaps [3]	afterwards [3]
I have to, I must [3]	I would like (to) [3]
open [3]	until [3]

3 más tarde	3 los huevos
3 bastante	3 ayer
3 quién	3 un periódico
4 el agua	4 alguien
4 arriba	4 delante (de)
4 detrás (de)	4 el pescado

3	3
the eggs	later
3	3
yesterday	enough
3	3
a newspaper	who
4	4
someone	the water
4	4
in front of	above, upstairs
4	4
the fish	behind

4	4
está bien	cómo
la salida	me gusta
nadie	nuestro
seguro	terminado
un resfriado	un vaso
una cosa	venir

how	it's all right
4	**4**
I like	the exit
4	**4**
our	nobody
4	**4**
finished	sure
4	**4**
a glass	a cold
4	**4**
(to) come	a thing, matter

la estación **5**	venga **5**
la parada **5**	allí **5**
abajo **5**	el buzón **5**
hacer **5**	por qué **5**
lleno **5**	el otro, la otra **5**
el coche **5**	la calle **5**

5 come, come on!	**5** the station
5 there	**5** the stop
5 the letterbox	**5** below, downstairs
5 why	**5** (to) make, do
5 the other	**5** full
5 the street	**5** the car

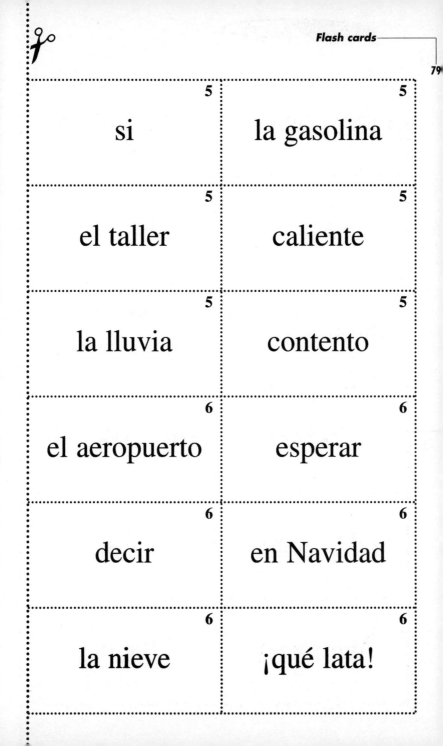

5 si	**5** la gasolina
5 el taller	**5** caliente
5 la lluvia	**5** contento
6 el aeropuerto	**6** esperar
6 decir	**6** en Navidad
6 la nieve	**6** ¡qué lata!

5 the petrol	**5** if
5 hot	**5** the mechanic
5 pleased	**5** the rain
6 (to) wait	**6** the airport
6 at Christmas	**6** (to) say
6 what a bore!	**6** the snow

6	6
¡hombre!	¿Le importaría?

6	6
veo	nunca

6	6
¿qué pasa?	¡espere!

6	6
el piso	sé

6	6
saber	la gente

6	6
llamar	conocemos

would you mind?	well, hello!
never	I see
wait!	What is the matter?
I know	the flat, apartment
the people	(to) know
we know	to call

Vamos a Madrid. 1

He estado en Marbella. 1

para mi empresa 1

Tengo una casa. 1

Tenemos dos niños. 1

Voy a casa. 1

Trabajo en Londres. 1

He trabajado mucho años. 1

El trabajo es bueno. 1

¿Está de vacaciones? 1

We go / let's go to Madrid. [1]

I have been / I was in Marbella. [1]

for my company [1]

I have a house. [1]

We have two children. [1]

I go, am going home. [1]

I work in London. [1]

I worked, have worked
many years. [1]

The work is good. [1]

Are you / Is he, she on holiday? [1]

¿Tiene usted una habitación?[2]

¿Dónde está la cafetería?[2]

¿Cuánto cuesta?[2]

¿Hay un banco aquí?[2]

Quisiéramos ir a Marbella.[2]

a las diez y media[2]

la cuenta, por favor[2]

Tengo una tarjeta de crédito.[2]

No puedo ir.[2]

¿A qué hora podemos comer?[2]

Do you have a room? [2]

Where is the café? [2]

How much does it cost? [2]

Is there a bank here? [2]

We would like to go to Marbella. [2]

at half past ten [2]

the bill, please [2]

I have a credit card. [2]

I cannot go. [2]

At what time can we eat? [2]

Voy de compras.

3

Tengo que ir de compras.

3

Hace mal tiempo.

3

Lo siento.

3

He comprado demasiado.

3

No importa.

3

Quisiera comprar…

3

He ido al supermercado.

3

Tenemos que comprar…

3

¿Ha visto…?

3

I am going shopping. 3

I must go shopping. 3

It is bad weather. 3

I am sorry. 3

I have bought too much. 3

It does not matter. 3

I would like to buy… 3

I have gone to the supermarket. 3

We have to buy… 3

Have you seen? 3

Alguien ha llamado. 4

No ha dicho para qué. 4

Es una cosa importante. 4

La semana que viene
tenemos tiempo. 4

Eso es posible. 4

Me gusta mucho. 4

El ajo no me gusta. 4

¿Le gusta el hotel? 4

¿Podría ayudarme, por favor? 4

¿Cómo se dice en español? 4

Someone has called. 4

He did not say why. 4

It is an important matter. 4

We have time next week. 4

That is possible. 4

I like it very much. 4

I do not like garlic. 4

Do you like the hotel? 4

Can you help me please? 4

How do you say in Spanish…? 4

dos billetes de ida y vuelta ⁵

Hable más despacio, por favor. ⁵

¿Cuándo hay un tren? ⁵

Voy a hacer algo. ⁵

Estoy muy contento/a. ⁵

Esperamos que sí. ⁵

¿Dónde está la carretera? ⁵

¿Por qué lo compra? ⁵
¡porque me gusta!

Hablo sólo un poco español. ⁵

Si hay un coche lo tenemos. ⁵

two return tickets

5

Please speak more slowly.

5

When is there a train?

5

I am going to do something.

5

I am very happy.

5

We hope so.

5

Where is the main road?

5

Why are you buying it?
Because I like it!

5

I only speak a little Spanish.

5

If there is a car we'll have it.

5

¿Qué tal sus vacaciones?

6

¿Le importaría ayudarme?

6

¿Le importaría darme…?

6

¿Qué pasa con…?

6

¡Vamos a tomar una copa!

6

No he ido nunca a Barcelona.

6

Tenemos que trabajar. ¡Qué lata!

6

He esperado durante una semana.

6

¿Qué ha hecho?

6

Tienen un piso. Lo sé.

6

How are your holidays? 6

Would you mind helping me? 6

Would you mind giving me…? 6

What's the matter with…? 6

Let's go and have a drink! 6

I never went to Barcelona. 6

We must work. What a bore! 6

I waited for a week. 6

What did you do? 6

They have a flat. I know that. 6

This is to certify
that

....

has successfully completed
a six week course of

Instant Spanish

with .... *results*

Date   *Instructor*